A Word About Weight Watchers

Since 1963, Weight Watchers has grown from a handful of people to millions of members annually. Today, Weight Watchers is recognized as one of the leading names in safe and sensible weight control. Weight Watchers members form a diverse group, from youths to senior citizens, attending meetings around the globe.

Although weight-loss and weight-management results vary by individual, we recommend that you attend Weight Watchers meetings, follow the Weight Watchers food plan, and participate in regular physical activity. For the Weight Watchers meetings nearest you, call 1-800-651-6000. Visit our Web site at WeightWatchers.com.

Fireside
Rockefeller Center
1230 Avenue of the Americas
New York, NY 10020

First Fireside Edition 2003

FIRESIDE and colophon are registered trademarks of Simon & Schuster, Inc.

WEIGHT WATCHERS is a registered trademark of Weight Watchers International, Inc.

For information regarding special discounts for bulk purchases, please contact Simon & Schuster Special Sales at 1-800-456-6798 or business@simonandschuster.com

Editorial and art produced by W/W Twentyfirst Corp.,
747 Third Avenue, New York, NY 10017.

Manufactured in the United States of America
10 9 8 7 6
Library of Congress Cataloging-in-Publication Data
Best of Weight Watchers magazine : over 145 tasty favorites—all 9 points or less / Weight Watchers International.
— 1st Fireside ed.
        p.   cm.
    "A Fireside book."
    Includes index.
      1. Reducing diets—Recipes. I. Weight Watchers International. II. Weight
    Watchers magazine.
RM222.2 .B4578 2003
641.5'635—dc21   2002042803
ISBN 0-7432-4595-4

Recipe symbols: 🍲 One Pot   🔥 Hot/Fiery

BEST OF
Weight Watchers
MAGAZINE
Over 145 Tasty Favorites—All 9 Points® or Less

VOLUME 1

WEIGHT WATCHERS INTERNATIONAL

A FIRESIDE BOOK
Published by Simon & Schuster
New York London Toronto Sydney

CONTENTS

STARTERS

It's your pick—
soothing sips,
get-up-and-go breakfasts,
or tasty bites
to whet the appetite!

Banana-Mango Smoothies

If you would like to serve more than two drinks, double or triple the ingredients—but don't try to make more than one batch at a time, or the blender may overflow.

1 mango, peeled and seeded
1 banana, peeled
1 cup ice cubes
⅔ cup pineapple juice
1 tablespoon fresh lime juice
2 teaspoons sugar
Mango and lime wedges (optional)

Combine the mango, banana, ice cubes, pineapple juice, lime juice, and sugar in a blender. Pulse on high speed until the mixture is thick and smooth. Pour the smoothie into 2 glasses and garnish with mango and lime wedges (if using).

Per serving (1¼ cups): 186 Cal, 1 g Fat, 0 g Sat Fat, 0 mg Chol, 4 mg Sod, 48 g Carb, 3 g Fib, 1 g Prot, 29 mg Calc. **POINTS: 3.**

SMART TIP

To turn this smoothie into a devilishly delectable cocktail, simply add 2 ounces of rum or vodka to the blender and pulse to mix all the ingredients. (Add 2 *POINTS* per serving.)

Hazelnut Coffee Shake

The stronger the coffee, the better this shake will taste, so splurge and break out your finest blend of java.

½ cup low-fat (1%) milk
½ cup sugar-free vanilla nonfat frozen yogurt
¼ cup brewed hazelnut coffee, chilled
3 ice cubes
½ teaspoon superfine sugar
¼ teaspoon cinnamon

Combine all the ingredients in a blender; until smooth. Pour into a chilled tall glass; sprinkle with additional cinnamon, if you like.

Per serving: 157 Cal, 1 g Fat, 1 g Sat Fat, 5 mg Chol, 116 mg Sod, 31 g Carb, 0 g Fib, 8 g Prot, 286 mg Calc. **POINTS: 3.**

SMART TIP

If instant dissolving superfine sugar isn't handy, use granulated sugar as a substitute.

Cranberry-Apple Cooler

MAKES 4 SERVINGS

Add a splash of sparkling water, and this brisk-tasting brew becomes a fabulous spritzer.

1½ cups low-calorie
    cranberry juice
    cocktail
1 cup brewed apple-
    spice tea, cooled
1 cup brewed black
    tea, cooled
½ cup orange juice
Thinly sliced oranges
    and/or lemons
    (optional)

Combine the cranberry juice cocktail, apple-spice and black teas, and orange juice; chill and serve over ice, garnishing with orange and/or lemon slices (if using).

Per serving (1¼ cups): 33 Cal, 0 g Fat, 0 g Sat Fat, 0 mg Chol, 6 mg Sod, 8 g Carb, 0 g Fib, 0 g Prot, 13 mg Calc. **POINTS: 1.**

SMART TIP

  To cool the hot brewed tea quickly, place in small bowl or glass measure and set in a larger bowl of ice water.

Rhubarb Iced Tea

MAKES 4 SERVINGS

The slight astringency of the fresh rhubarb makes this refreshing summer beverage especially thirst-quenching. It's also a favorite with kids, who love the bright pink color.

3 cups chopped
    rhubarb
    (¼-inch pieces)
3 cups water
2 tablespoons honey
1 cinnamon stick
1–3 tablespoons fresh
    lemon juice
Mint or lavender sprigs
    (optional)

1. Place the rhubarb, water, honey, and cinnamon stick in a large stainless steel saucepan; bring to a boil. Reduce the heat, and simmer 15 minutes, removing the cinnamon stick after 10 minutes. Remove from the heat and let steep 1 hour.
2. Pour through a fine strainer into a large pitcher, without squeezing (it will become cloudy). Refrigerate until chilled through, at least 2 hours. Stir in the lemon juice to taste. Serve over ice in chilled tall glasses, adding water to fill and garnishing with mint or lavender (if using).

Per serving (½ cup): 33 Cal, 0 g Fat, 0 g Sat Fat, 0 mg Chol, 2 mg Sod, 9 g Carb, 0 g Fib, 0 g Prot, 5 mg Calc. **POINTS: 1.**

SMART TIP

  Sweeten this refresher with your favorite variety of honey—clover, orange blossom, or lavender.

weight watchers

Orange Muffins with Apricots and Cranberries

MAKES 12 SERVINGS

For a fresh twist on the morning muffin, juice any variety of orange on hand—navel, temple, or Valencia. Use a thick-handled wooden spoon to stir this stiff and sticky batter.

- 1 cup all-purpose flour
- ¾ cup whole-wheat flour
- ¼ cup wheat germ
- 2 teaspoons baking powder
- ½ teaspoon baking soda
- ¼ teaspoon salt
- 4 tablespoons (½ stick) unsalted butter or margarine, cut into small cubes
- ½ cup sugar
- ⅔ cup orange juice
- 1 large egg
- 1 cup sweetened dried cranberries
- 1 cup chopped dried apricot halves

1. Preheat the oven to 350°F. Spray a 12-cup muffin tin with nonstick spray or line with foil or paper liners.

2. Combine the all-purpose flour, whole-wheat flour, wheat germ, baking powder, baking soda, and salt in a bowl. With a fork or your fingers, combine the butter with the dry ingredients until the mixture is crumbly. Stir in the sugar.

3. Combine the orange juice and egg in another bowl. Add the juice mixture to the flour mixture; stir just until blended. The dough will be very stiff. Stir in the cranberries and apricots.

4. Spoon the batter into the cups, filling each about three-quarters full. Bake until the surface of the muffins is golden brown, or until a toothpick inserted in a muffin comes out clean, 20–25 minutes. Cool in the pan on a rack 5 minutes; remove from the pan and cool completely on the rack.

Per serving (1 muffin): 211 Cal, 5 g Fat, 3 g Sat Fat, 29 mg Chol, 216 mg Sod, 39 g Carb, 3 g Fib, 4 g Prot, 27 mg Calc. **POINTS: 4.**

SMART TIP

For a more intense orange flavor, add two teaspoons grated orange rind to the batter when folding in the cranberries and apricots.

Maple-Pear Oatmeal Muffins

These sweet muffins taste best if you use a Bosc, Bartlett, or Anjou pear—just make sure it is firm but ripe.

1¾ cups all-purpose flour
1 teaspoon baking soda
1 teaspoon baking powder
1 teaspoon cinnamon
½ teaspoon salt
2 tablespoons finely chopped pecans
1½ cups quick-cooking rolled oats
1 large pear, cored, peeled, and chopped
1 cup fat-free buttermilk
½ cup packed dark brown sugar
⅓ cup pure maple syrup
2 tablespoons vegetable oil
1 large egg

1. Preheat the oven to 400°F. Spray a 12-cup muffin tin with nonstick spray or line with foil or paper liners.
2. Combine the flour, baking soda, baking powder, cinnamon, and salt in one bowl. Combine the pecans and 2 tablespoons of the oats in another bowl. Combine the remaining oats, the pear, buttermilk, brown sugar, syrup, oil, and egg in a bowl; let stand 5 minutes. Add the oat-pear mixture to the flour mixture; stir just until blended.
3. Spoon the batter into the cups, filling each about two-thirds full. Sprinkle tops with the pecan-oat mixture. Bake until a toothpick inserted in a muffin comes out clean, 18–20 minutes. Cool in the pan on a rack 5 minutes; remove from the pan and cool completely on the rack.

Per serving (1 muffin): 220 Cal, 5 g Fat, 1 g Sat Fat, 18 mg Chol, 256 mg Sod, 40 g Carb, 2 g Fib, 5 g Prot, 60 mg Calc. **POINTS: 4.**

SMART TIP

The muffins will keep stored in an airtight container at room temperature for up to three days.

starters

Classic Scones

Serve these scones warmed, split, and filled with raspberries, alongside a cup of coffee or your favorite tea. Dried fruits are wonderful mixed into the scone batter, but don't forget to add in the extra **POINTS**.

1 cup + 2 tablespoons all-purpose flour

1 tablespoon sugar

1 teaspoon baking powder

¼ teaspoon baking soda

¼ teaspoon salt

½ cup plain low-fat yogurt

1 large egg

1 tablespoon margarine, melted and cooled

1. Preheat the oven to 425°F. Spray a baking sheet with nonstick spray.

2. Combine the flour, sugar, baking powder, baking soda, and salt in a bowl. Combine the yogurt, egg, and margarine in another bowl. Add the yogurt mixture to the flour mixture; stir just until blended.

3. On a lightly floured counter, roll out the dough into a ¼-inch-thick round. With a sharp knife, cut the dough into 12 wedges. Arrange the wedges on the baking sheet. Reduce the oven temperature to 400°F. Bake until the scones are golden brown, 12–15 minutes. Cool on a wire rack 10 minutes.

Per serving (1 scone): 70 Cal, 2 g Fat, 0 g Sat Fat, 19 mg Chol, 135 mg Sod, 11 g Carb, 0 g Fib, 3 g Prot, 67 mg Calc. **POINTS: 2.**

SMART TIP

Lightly sprinkle the knife with flour so the dough cuts more easily into wedges.

Breakfast Kebabs

These yummy, fruity kebabs won't soon be forgotten, especially when served alongside a waffle or a pancake. If using wooden skewers be sure to soak them in water for at least 30 minutes before cooking.

1 tablespoon fruit juice

1 tablespoon maple syrup

4 turkey breakfast sausages, cut into thirds

1 apple, cored and cut into chunks

½ cup cubed fresh pineapple

1. Combine the fruit juice and syrup in a small bowl. Thread the sausages, apple, and pineapple onto 4 skewers, alternating the ingredients. Brush with the juice mixture. Refrigerate, covered, until ready to cook.

2. Spray the broiler or grill rack with nonstick spray; preheat the broiler, or prepare the grill. Cook the kebabs, 5 inches from heat, until the sausages are cooked through and the fruit is tender, about 4 minutes on each side.

Per serving (2 skewers): 168 Cal, 6 g Fat, 2 g Sat Fat, 15 mg Chol, 202 mg Sod, 22 g Carb, 2 g Fib, 5 g Prot, 38 mg Calc. **POINTS: 3.**

SMART TIP

When preparing kebabs, cut the ingredients into uniform-size chunks. The ingredients can be set out so kids will have fun helping to thread the skewers.

14

starters

Bagel Crisps with Cream Cheese–Olive Spread

These bagel crisps are so yummy, you may find your family clamoring for them in the morning as well as at snack time.

2 small bagels

½ cup fat-free cream cheese

3 tablespoons chopped stuffed green olives

2 teaspoons olive brine

1 tablespoon snipped chives or thinly sliced scallion tops

1. Preheat the oven to 300°F. Slice the bagels in half into 2 rounds; slice each round in half again to make 4 thin rounds. Place the bagel rounds on a nonstick baking sheet; toast, turning once, until golden brown, about 10 minutes.

2. Meanwhile, combine the cream cheese, olives, brine, and chives in a small bowl. Spread 1 tablespoon of the cheese-olive spread on each bagel crisp and serve warm.

Per serving (2 bagel crisps): 97 Cal, 1 g Fat, 0 g Sat Fat, 0 mg Chol, 342 mg Sod, 16 g Carb, 1 g Fib, 6 g Prot, 36 mg Calc. **POINTS: 2.**

SMART TIP

This is a great way to use leftover bagels—but take care to cut them with a serrated knife.

Tortilla Egg Roll-Ups

MAKES 4 SERVINGS

This is a way to have the flavor of huevos rancheros—the Southwestern breakfast favorite—without all the calories.

½ green bell pepper, seeded and chopped

3 scallions, thinly sliced

1 plum tomato, chopped

4 large eggs

4 egg whites

½ teaspoon salt

½ teaspoon hot pepper sauce

4 (6-inch) fat-free flour tortillas

½ cup shredded reduced-fat sharp cheddar cheese

1 tablespoon chopped fresh cilantro

1. Spray a large nonstick skillet with nonstick spray and set over medium-high heat. Add the bell pepper and cook until tender-crisp, about 3 minutes. Add the scallions and tomato; sauté until softened, about 1 minute. Transfer the vegetables to a plate.

2. Beat the eggs, egg whites, salt, and pepper sauce together in a medium bowl. Spray the skillet with more nonstick spray and set over medium-high heat. Add the egg mixture and cook, stirring as needed, until the eggs are scrambled but not dry. Remove from the heat and gently toss the eggs with the sautéed vegetables.

3. Heat the tortillas according to the package directions. Fill the tortillas by spooning one-fourth of the egg-vegetable mixture along the bottom edge of each tortilla; sprinkle each with some cheese and cilantro. Roll up the tortillas tightly, then cut them in half and serve.

Per serving (1 roll-up): 201 Cal, 8 g Fat, 3 g Sat Fat, 222 mg Chol, 706 mg Sod, 16 g Carb, 7 g Fib, 17 g Prot, 181 mg Calc. **POINTS: 4.**

SMART TIP

If you want to tame the heat, reduce the hot pepper sauce to ¼ teaspoon.

Fruit-Filled Breakfast Wontons

Don't be put off by the name—these fruity wontons are surprisingly easy to make and will be snapped up by those with a sweet tooth. If you have any leftovers, store them in an airtight container for up to two days.

8 square wonton
  skins
¼ cup golden raisins
4 large walnut halves,
  cut in half
1 tablespoon packed
  brown sugar
⅛ teaspoon cinnamon

1. Preheat the oven to 400°F; line a baking sheet with foil and spray with nonstick spray. Bring a large pot of water to a simmer.

2. Place the wonton skins on a work surface; moisten the edges with water. Place a few raisins and one walnut piece in the center of each wonton skin; fold the wontons in half diagonally, pressing the edges to seal tightly.

3. Place the wontons in the simmering water for about 1 minute. With a slotted spoon, transfer the wontons to paper towels to drain. Arrange the wontons on the baking sheet.

4. Combine the brown sugar and cinnamon in a bowl and sprinkle over the wontons. Bake until the wontons are lightly browned and crisp, 8–10 minutes.

Per serving (2 wontons): 104 Cal, 2 g Fat, 0 g Sat Fat, 1 mg Chol, 94 mg Sod, 21 g Carb, 1 g Fib, 2 g Prot, 19 mg Calc. **POINTS: 2.**

SMART TIP

Try making wontons the night before with any young cooks in your family; children will enjoy filling and sealing them.

Zucchini Omelet with Croutons

MAKES 1 SERVING

For an extra fiber touch, use whole-grain or high-fiber bread instead of white. To make a more colorful omelet, use equal amounts of shredded green and yellow zucchini.

½ teaspoon olive oil
1 garlic clove, lightly crushed
1 slice reduced-calorie white bread, cubed
1 large egg, lightly beaten
½ cup shredded zucchini
1 teaspoon grated Parmesan cheese
Pinch salt
Pinch ground white pepper
2 teaspoons water

1. Heat a small nonstick skillet over medium heat. Swirl in the oil, then add the garlic. Cook, stirring constantly, until the garlic clove softens. Add the bread cubes to the skillet; cook, stirring constantly, until golden brown. Set aside.

2. Combine the egg, zucchini, cheese, salt, pepper, and the water in a small bowl; pour into another nonstick skillet, tilting it to cover the bottom of the pan with the egg mixture. Cook over medium heat until the underside of the omelet is set, lifting the edges with a spatula to let the uncooked egg flow underneath, 1½ minutes. Turn the omelet over with a spatula; continue to cook until firm, 1 minute.

3. Sprinkle the croutons over half of the omelet; then use the spatula to fold the other half over the filling. Cook until the croutons are heated, 30 seconds. Slide the omelet onto a plate.

Per serving: 164 Cal, 8 g Fat, 2 g Sat Fat, 214 mg Chol, 333 mg Sod, 14 g Carb, 2 g Fib, 10 g Prot, 86 mg Calc. **POINTS: 4.**

SMART TIP

Be sure to start with a clean pan when making omelets, or your eggs will stick. It's important to always store eggs large-end up, since it keeps them fresh and helps yolks stay centered. Never place eggs near odoriferous foods (such as onions) because they can easily absorb the smell.

starters

Shrimp in Garlic Sauce

MAKES 6 SERVINGS

This simple starter can be found on the menu of almost any Spanish restaurant, here and abroad. The key to this dish is a quick sauté over fairly high heat. The addition of fresh parsley at the end helps mellow the garlic.

2 teaspoons extra-virgin olive oil

1 onion, finely chopped

3 garlic cloves, minced

¾ pound medium shrimp, peeled and deveined

¾ teaspoon paprika

½ teaspoon ground cumin

½ teaspoon salt

2 tablespoons dry sherry

1 tablespoon fresh lemon juice

¼ cup chopped fresh parsley

Heat a large nonstick skillet over medium–high heat. Swirl in the oil, then add the onion and garlic. Cook until the onion and garlic begin to soften, 3–4 minutes. Add the shrimp, paprika, cumin, and salt; cook, stirring occasionally, just until the shrimp are opaque, about 4 minutes. Add the sherry and lemon juice, and cook 1 minute longer. Remove from the heat and stir in the parsley. Serve warm or at room temperature.

Per serving (½ cup): 70 Cal, 2 g Fat, 0 g Sat Fat, 81 mg Chol, 290 mg Sod, 3 g Carb, 1 g Fib, 9 g Prot, 29 mg Calc. **POINTS: 1.**

SMART TIP

This dish is even more flavorful when made in advance. Cook the shrimp through, then refrigerate until chilled, at least one hour or up to a day ahead. Bring to room temperature, then toss with the parsley and serve.

MINUTE APPETIZERS

The next time you find yourself entertaining unexpected guests, wow them with this appetizer spread (little to no assembly required):
Thin slices of prosciutto or high-quality deli ham wrapped around precut chunks of ripe melon and held together with a toothpick
Roasted red peppers from the deli or a jar
Homemade bean salad Mix one 15-ounce can cannellini (white kidney) beans, tossed with one 2-ounce can drained, olive-oil-packed solid white tuna
Marinated artichokes from the deli or a jar
Grape tomatoes, halved and drizzled with low-fat vinaigrette
Canned smoked oysters or mussels
Stuffed green olives Try anchovy- or tuna-stuffed, available in Latino and gourmet grocery stores

Spicy Red Peppers

MAKES 6 SERVINGS

These savory strips are fabulous on sliced crusty bread, and they make any salad special. Roast a double batch when red bell peppers are on sale; they'll last up to a week in the refrigerator and up to a month in the freezer. For best flavor, omit the lemon rind when preparing the peppers for freezing, then add it to the thawed peppers just before serving. To freeze the peppers, place them in a zip-close freezer bag and squeeze out as much air as possible. Thaw overnight in the refrigerator.

4 red bell peppers
1 teaspoon extra-virgin olive oil
2 garlic cloves, thinly sliced
¼ teaspoon crushed red pepper
¼ teaspoon salt
½ teaspoon grated lemon rind

1. Preheat the oven to 425°F. Spray a baking sheet with nonstick spray.
2. Arrange the peppers on the baking sheet and roast 15 minutes. Turn the peppers and roast until they are softened and blistered, about 15 minutes longer. Transfer the peppers to a large bowl. Cover the bowl with plastic wrap, and steam 15 minutes. When cool enough to handle, peel, core, and seed the peppers, reserving the remaining juice in the bowl, and cut them into ½-inch-wide strips.
3. Heat a nonstick skillet over medium-high heat. Swirl in the oil, then add the garlic. Cook, stirring occasionally, 1 minute. Add the pepper strips, crushed red pepper, and salt; cook 3–4 minutes. Add the reserved pepper juice and cook 1 minute longer. Remove from the heat and stir in the grated lemon rind. Serve warm or at room temperature.

Per serving (⅓ cup): 22 Cal, 1 g Fat, 0 g Sat Fat, 4 mg Chol, 98 mg Sod, 4 g Carb, 1 g Fib, 1 g Prot, 6 mg Calc. **POINTS: 0.**

SMART TIP

This recipe makes wise use of the juices created by roasting peppers—a clever idea anytime. Roasted-pepper juices add wonderful flavor and body to salad dressings and are also tasty in poultry or vegetable marinades.

Cerveza-Marinated Chicken Skewers

MAKES 6 SERVINGS

Cerveza, the Spanish word for beer, adds a malty tang to spicy grilled chicken. Cook the chicken on a ridged grill pan or in the broiler if you don't feel like firing up the outdoor grill.

1 cup beer
2 tablespoons fresh lemon juice
1 tablespoon extra-virgin olive oil
1 teaspoon paprika
1 teaspoon dried oregano
1 teaspoon salt
Freshly ground pepper, to taste
1 pound skinless boneless chicken breast halves, cut into 1-inch chunks

1. Combine the beer, lemon juice, oil, paprika, oregano, salt, and pepper in a zip-close plastic bag; add the chicken. Squeeze out the air and seal the bag; turn to coat the chicken. Refrigerate 1 hour, turning the bag occasionally.

2. Transfer the marinade to a small saucepan and bring to a boil. Reduce the heat to low and simmer, 5 minutes.

3. If using wooden skewers, soak them in hot water 30 minutes (to prevent them from burning).

4. Spray the broiler or grill rack with nonstick spray; preheat. (Or spray a nonstick ridged grill pan with nonstick spray and set over high heat.)

5. Divide the chicken among 12 (8-inch) skewers (about 2 chunks apiece). Grill or broil the skewers 4 inches from heat until lightly browned, about 3 minutes; turn and brush with the reduced marinade. Cook 3 minutes longer, turn and brush with the marinade again. Cook until the chicken is cooked through, about 2 more minutes. Serve immediately.

Per serving (2 skewers): 108 Cal, 3 g Fat, 1 g Sat Fat, 41 mg Chol, 233 mg Sod, 1 g Carb, 0 g Fib, 16 g Prot, 12 mg Calc. **POINTS: 2.**

SMART TIP

> You can also serve these tasty morsels as a main-dish salad for four: Just toss the cooked chicken with about six cups of crunchy greens (pick your favorite prewashed, bagged blend in the produce aisle) and drizzle with a little sherry vinegar and olive oil.

weight watchers

Marinated Artichokes

MAKES 6 SERVINGS

To lightly crush the fennel seeds in this recipe, place them in a zip-close plastic bag and tap them several times with a rolling pin or can.

2 (14-ounce) cans artichoke hearts, drained and quartered

2 medium oranges, peeled and cut into segments

1 tablespoon sherry vinegar

2 teaspoons extra-virgin olive oil

1 teaspoon grated orange rind

$\frac{1}{2}$ teaspoon ground cumin

$\frac{1}{2}$ teaspoon dried oregano

$\frac{1}{2}$ teaspoon fennel seeds, lightly crushed

$\frac{1}{4}$ teaspoon salt

Combine all of the ingredients in a medium glass, ceramic, or stainless steel bowl. Let marinate at room temperature 4 hours or in the refrigerator overnight.

Per serving (½ cup): 86 Cal, 2 g Fat, 0 g Sat Fat, 0 mg Chol, 389 mg Sod, 17 g Carb, 6 g Fib, 4 g Prot, 66 mg Calc. **POINTS: 1.**

SMART TIP

When you grate the orange rind, capture only the rind—the orange skin—and none of the bitter white pith underneath. Grate the whole orange, then wrap the remaining rind tightly in plastic wrap and freeze—you'll always have an instant flavor booster on hand.

SMART SUBSTITUTIONS

Some of the most frequently ordered appetizers served in restaurants have fat and calorie counts to match their popularity. Try these healthier substitutes and save valuable **POINTS**.

Instead of:	Try:
4 cheese nachos **8 POINTS**	12 tortilla chips with ½ cup pico de gallo **4 POINTS**
3 Buffalo wings **9 POINTS**	4 small stuffed mushrooms **3 POINTS**
½ cup fried calamari **11 POINTS**	1 slice of bruschetta **3 POINTS**
1 beef egg roll **5 POINTS**	3 Chinese pancakes **3 POINTS**

Figs Wrapped in Ham

MAKES 6 SERVINGS

This appetizer combines the sweet taste of dried figs with the salty bite of ham. It's a great do-ahead choice: Prepare the figs to the point of baking, then cover them with plastic wrap and refrigerate for a few hours or overnight. When ready to use, simply uncover and bake as directed.

18 dried figs
 1 cup orange juice
 2 tablespoons sherry vinegar
18 whole blanched almonds
 2 ounces deli-sliced boiled ham, cut lengthwise into 18 (¾-inch-wide) strips

1. Preheat the oven to 400°F. Spray a baking sheet with nonstick spray.

2. Combine the figs, orange juice, and vinegar in a medium saucepan. Bring to a boil over high heat and cook 1 minute. Remove from the heat and let stand until the figs are softened, 10 minutes. Drain, discarding any remaining liquid, and let cool 5 minutes.

3. With the tip of a sharp knife, make a ¾-inch incision in each fig. Place one almond into each fig. Working one at a time, roll a ham strip around a fig and place seam-side down on the baking sheet. Repeat with the remaining figs. Bake until the ham begins to brown slightly and the figs are hot, 10–12 minutes. Serve immediately or at room temperature.

Per serving (3 figs): 201 Cal, 3 g Fat, 1 g Sat Fat, 6 mg Chol, 149 mg Sod, 42 g Carb, 6 g Fib, 5 g Prot, 95 mg Calc. **POINTS: 3.**

SMART TIP

For a nuttier flavor, toast the almonds in a small skillet over medium heat until fragrant, about 1 minute, before stuffing the figs.

Shrimp with Cilantro Mojo on Tortilla Crisps

MAKES 6 SERVINGS

Mojo, a citrus-based sauce invented in Cuba, can be used both as a marinade and as an accompaniment for cooked meats, fish, or poultry.

4 (6-inch) corn tortillas, each cut into 6 triangles
1 teaspoon salt
⅓ cup orange juice
¼ cup fresh lime juice
¼ cup fat-free chicken broth
3 garlic cloves, minced
4 teaspoons olive oil
1 teaspoon sugar
1 teaspoon dried oregano
¼ cup chopped fresh cilantro
1 pound (about 24) large shrimp, peeled and deveined

1. Preheat the oven to 350°F. Arrange tortilla triangles on a jelly-roll pan in a single layer. Lightly coat the tortillas with nonstick spray and sprinkle with ¼ teaspoon of the salt. Bake until tortillas are crisp and lightly browned around the edges, about 6–7 minutes; set aside.

2. Combine the orange juice, lime juice, chicken broth, garlic, 3 teaspoons of the oil, the sugar, ½ teaspoon of the remaining salt, and the oregano in a small saucepan. Bring the mixture to a boil, reduce the heat, and simmer 5 minutes. Remove from the heat, stir in the cilantro, and cool 5 minutes. Reserve ¼ cup of the mojo and set aside. Pour the remaining mojo into a medium bowl and add the shrimp, tossing well to coat. Let the shrimp marinate 15 minutes.

3. Drain the shrimp, season with the remaining ¼ teaspoon salt, and discard the marinade. Heat a large nonstick skillet over medium-high heat. Swirl in the remaining 1 teaspoon oil, then add the shrimp. Cook until opaque, about 2–3 minutes per side; remove from the heat. Arrange each shrimp on a tortilla crisp and drizzle with the reserved mojo sauce.

Per serving (4 tortilla crisps): 119 Cal, 3 g Fat, 0 g Sat Fat, 120 mg Chol, 562 mg Sod, 9 g Carb, 1 g Fib, 14 g Prot, 57 mg Calc. **POINTS: 2.**

SMART TIP

To peel and devein shrimp, cut the shell with kitchen scissors or a small knife, following the curve of the outer back and moving from the top toward the tail to expose the dark vein. Place shrimp under cold running water while removing the shell and the vein.

Spanish Potato Tortilla

MAKES 6 SERVINGS

Cut this savory omelet into wedges and serve warm or make the recipe up to
one day ahead (wrap it in plastic wrap and refrigerate), then serve at room temperature.
For a striking presentation, garnish with habañero peppers (but don't eat them).

1¾ pounds russet
   potatoes, peeled
   and sliced into thin
   rounds
4 teaspoons
   extra-virgin olive oil
1 large onion, sliced
4 large eggs
4 egg whites
1 teaspoon salt
Freshly ground pepper,
   to taste

1. Place the potato slices in a large pot and add enough water to cover them by 1 inch. Bring to a boil; reduce the heat and simmer until the potatoes are just tender, about 3 minutes. Drain and let cool 5 minutes.

2. Meanwhile, heat a large nonstick skillet over medium heat. Swirl in 1 teaspoon of the oil, then add the onion. Cook until softened but not browned, 5–6 minutes. Remove from the heat and set aside.

3. Whisk the eggs, egg whites, salt, and pepper in a medium bowl. Add the warm potatoes and onion, mixing well to coat; let stand 15 minutes. Return the skillet to medium-high heat. Swirl in the remaining 3 teaspoons oil, then add the potato-egg mixture, patting with a spatula to form a disk. Cook undisturbed 3 minutes; reduce the heat to medium and cook until the tortilla is golden on the bottom, about 8 minutes longer. Invert a large plate over the skillet and flip the skillet over to drop the tortilla onto the plate. Return the skillet to the heat and slide the tortilla back into the pan, uncooked side down. Cook until the bottom is golden, about 5 minutes.

4. Meanwhile, wash the plate in hot, soapy water (to prevent bacterial contamination from the raw eggs).

5. Invert the plate over the skillet again and flip the skillet over to drop the tortilla onto the plate. Slide the tortilla back into the pan and cook about 5 minutes longer. Remove from the heat; let cool 10 minutes before serving.

Per serving (⅙ of tortilla): 200 Cal, 7 g Fat, 1 g Sat Fat, 142 mg Chol, 473 mg Sod, 27 g Carb, 3 g Fib, 9 g Prot, 33 mg Calc. *POINTS: 4.*

SMART TIP

This recipe also makes a wonderful main dish for four on its own; serve it with a green salad or a side of crisp-cooked green beans dressed with vinaigrette.

starters

Goat Cheese–Stuffed Mushroom Caps with Fresh Herbs

MAKES 6 SERVINGS

Our stuffed mushroom caps have all the flavor—with none of the greasiness—usually found in this favorite. You can prepare the mushrooms up to one day ahead, refrigerate them, and then bake when ready to serve. For extra richness, add 1 tablespoon of finely chopped pecans to the herbed bread crumbs. (Add 1 **POINT** per serving.)

30 (1¾ pounds) cremini mushrooms, about 2 inches in diameter
2 tablespoons dry white wine
1 tablespoon fresh lemon juice
½ teaspoon kosher salt
Freshly ground pepper, to taste
½ cup shallots, minced
3 slices firm white bread, made into crumbs
3 teaspoons chopped fresh parsley
3 teaspoons chopped fresh cilantro
1 (2-ounce) log fresh goat cheese, crumbled

1. Preheat the oven to 400°F. Wash the mushrooms in a large bowl of water, lift them out, and drain them in a colander 15–20 minutes, tossing once or twice until dry. Trim off the bottom of the stems; carefully remove the stems and set aside.
2. Combine the wine, lemon juice, ¼ teaspoon of the salt, and are grinding of the pepper in a large bowl. Add the mushroom caps and toss until evenly coated. Spray a nonstick jelly-roll pan or baking sheet with nonstick spray. Arrange the mushroom caps on the pan, stem-side up. Lightly spray with nonstick spray. Bake until the caps are full of liquid, 8–10 minutes. Transfer the mushroom caps to a colander set over a bowl; drain and reserve the juices.
3. Spray a large nonstick skillet with nonstick spray and place over medium heat. Add the mushroom stems and the shallots; cook until the stems begin to release their juices, about 5 minutes. Add the remaining ¼ teaspoon salt, another grinding of the pepper, and the reserved mushroom juice. Cook until the mixture is almost dry, 6–7 minutes. Transfer the mixture to a bowl, loosely cover, and let cool to room temperature.
4. Coarsely chop the mushroom stem mixture in a food processor. Add half of the bread crumbs, 2 teaspoons of the parsley, 2 teaspoons of the cilantro, and the goat cheese. Pulse until the mixture is blended and the mushroom stems are finely chopped. Scrape the mixture into a bowl.
5. Combine the remaining bread crumbs with the remaining 1 teaspoon parsley and 1 teaspoon cilantro in a small bowl. Stuff each mushroom cap with ½ tablespoon of the goat cheese mixture. Arrange the mushroom caps on a nonstick jelly-roll pan or baking sheet, sprinkle with the herbed bread crumbs, and bake until golden brown and heated through, about 10 minutes.

Per serving (5 stuffed mushrooms): 107 Cal, 4 g Fat, 2 g Sat Fat, 9 mg Chol, 257 mg Sod, 14 g Carb, 2 g Fib, 6 g Prot, 76 mg Calc. **POINTS: 2.**

SUPER BOWLS

There's nothing more satisfying than
a great bowl of steaming soup or
stew, or crisp, refreshing salad. Check out the
tasty surprises simmering in the pot
and discover how easy it is to take the "blah"
out of a boring bowl of greens!

Tuscan Bread Salad

MAKES 4 SERVINGS

Here's our thoroughly modern take on the traditional recipe for Panzanella, a mix of tomatoes and bread. It's a classic Italian dish with a practical Italian approach to cooking: The recipe was created to make use of leftover bread and the abundance of summer tomatoes. Our version uses part-skim mozzarella cheese.

2 tablespoons low-sodium vegetable broth
1 tablespoon red-wine vinegar
2 teaspoons extra-virgin olive oil
½ teaspoon dried oregano
Pinch salt
Freshly ground pepper, to taste
4 slices stale crusty peasant bread, cubed (4 ounces)
4 tomatoes, chopped
⅔ cup part-skim mozzarella cheese, cut into thin strips
½ sweet onion, very thinly sliced
2 tablespoons minced fresh basil
2 tablespoons minced fresh flat-leaf parsley

1. Combine the broth, vinegar, oil, oregano, salt, and pepper in a small bowl.

2. Place the bread in a large bowl and sprinkle with enough water to moisten slightly, without turning the bread soggy. Add the tomatoes, cheese, onion, basil, and parsley; drizzle with the dressing and toss to coat. Let stand at least 30 minutes, but no more than 2 hours, to blend flavors.

Per serving (2 cups): 181 Cal, 7 g Fat, 2 g Sat Fat, 11 mg Chol, 312 mg Sod, 23 g Carb, 3 g Fib, 9 g Prot, 160 mg Calc. **POINTS: 4.**

SMART TIP

If you want to incorporate more soy into your diet, substitute extra-firm tofu for the cheese.

super bowls

Warm Sage-Potato Salad

MAKES 6 SERVINGS

Got a yen for something tasty and tangy? Douse spuds with some vinegar, but rather than reach for the oil, grab a handful of fresh herbs. Going on a picnic? Take this dish: It's mayoless, so there's no need to worrying about the dressing spoiling.

1¾ pounds new potatoes, rinsed
2 tablespoons Champagne vinegar
¼ teaspoon salt
½ teaspoon freshly ground pepper
2½ tablespoons chopped fresh chives
2 teaspoons chopped fresh sage

1. Place the potatoes in a saucepan with enough water to cover them, and then bring the water to a boil. Simmer until the potatoes are tender when pierced with a knife, about 20 minutes. Drain; let cool for 10 minutes.

2. Cut the potatoes in half (or quarters if potatoes are large) and place them in a bowl. Drizzle the potatoes with the vinegar and toss; add the salt and pepper. Sprinkle the chives and sage over the potatoes and gently toss until the seasonings are blended. Serve warm or at room temperature.

Per serving (½ cup): 116 Cal, 0 g Fat, 0 g Sat Fat, 0 mg Chol, 104 mg Sod, 26 g Carb, 2 g Fib, 3 g Prot, 16 mg Calc. **POINTS: 2.**

SMART TIP

If Champagne vinegar isn't handy, use white-wine vinegar as a substitute.

Radish-Orange Salad

MAKES 6 SERVINGS

This salad is cool, refreshing, and a bit sweet—a perfect side dish with a spicy barbecue.

3 small oranges
¼ cup fresh lime juice
1 tablespoon peanut oil
½ teaspoon ground coriander
Freshly ground pepper, to taste
1½ cups thinly sliced radishes
6 medium celery stalks, thinly sliced

1. Cut off the peel and white pith from each orange. Cut the oranges into 1-inch-thick slices, stack the slices, and cut them into quarters.

2. Combine the lime juice, oil, coriander, and pepper in a small bowl.

3. Combine the orange slices, the radishes, and celery in a bowl. Drizzle the dressing over oranges and vegetables, and toss gently to coat.

Per serving (1 cup): 61 Cal, 3 g Fat, 0 g Sat Fat, 0 mg Chol, 33 mg Sod, 10 g Carb, 3 g Fib, 1 g Prot, 46 mg Calc. **POINTS: 1.**

SMART TIP

You can substitute extra-virgin olive oil for the peanut oil with equally delicious results.

Carrot and Cucumber Salad

MAKES 4 SERVINGS

Transform this simple, refreshing salad into a main course by adding canned tuna or slices of cooked chicken; serve with whole-wheat crisp breads.

2 large cucumbers, peeled, halved lengthwise, seeded, and thinly sliced

2 carrots, peeled and thinly sliced on an angle

½ red onion, thinly sliced

2 tablespoons cider vinegar

1 tablespoon fresh lime juice

1 tablespoon sugar

1 tablespoon chopped fresh cilantro

½ teaspoon salt

¼ teaspoon freshly ground pepper

Combine all the ingredients in a bowl. Toss well and let stand 10 minutes before serving.

Per serving (1 cup): 55 Cal, 0 g Fat, 0 g Sat Fat, 0 mg Chol, 308 mg Sod, 13 g Carb, 3 g Fib, 2 g Prot, 35 mg Calc. **POINTS: 1.**

SMART TIP

To seed the cucumber, halve it lengthwise and scrape out the seeds with a small spoon.

super bowls

MARATHON SALAD

Use this clever technique—developed by food scientist Shirley Corriher, Ph.D., author of *Cookwise* (Morrow, 1997)—and your greens will stay fresh and salad-ready for several weeks. First, wash the greens in several changes of cold water. Tear them into bite-size pieces and let them soak in cold water for 30 minutes. Then dry them thoroughly in a salad spinner and blot off any excess water with paper towels. Place the leaves, with one or two sheets of paper towel, in a large zip-close plastic bag. Squeeze out as much air as possible and refrigerate. All that's left to do is toss in a few of our suggested fixings every time you use the lettuce. Top with a reduced-fat or fat-free dressing, and enjoy a different salad every night of the week.

SUNDAY

Add chunked, pared apples; chopped, toasted walnuts; and a sprinkling of crumbled blue cheese.

DRESSING SUGGESTION

Mustard vinaigrette

MONDAY

Add sliced strawberries, a mandarin orange, and a thinly sliced sweet onion.

DRESSING SUGGESTION

Whisk a little canola oil and orange juice with some minced onion and a pinch of dried thyme.

Herb-Tomato Salad

MAKES 4 SERVINGS

When the summer garden is teeming with fresh, ripe tomatoes, slice and dress them with this trio of Mediterranean herbs and tangy vinaigrette.

3 tablespoons red-wine vinegar

4 teaspoons extra-virgin olive oil

½ teaspoon sugar

½ teaspoon salt

½ teaspoon Dijon mustard

¼ teaspoon freshly ground pepper

4 tomatoes, sliced

1 red onion, thinly sliced and separated into rings

2 tablespoons chopped fresh parsley

1 tablespoon chopped fresh oregano

1 teaspoon chopped fresh thyme

1. Whisk the vinegar, oil, sugar, salt, mustard, and pepper together in a small bowl.

2. Arrange the tomatoes and onion rings on a plate; drizzle with dressing, and then sprinkle with the remaining herbs.

3. Cover with plastic wrap; let stand at room temperature 1 hour to allow the flavors to blend.

Per serving (1 cup): 81 Cal, 5 g Fat, 1 g Sat Fat, 0 mg Chol, 307 mg Sod, 9 g Carb, 2 g Fib, 2 g Prot, 19 mg Calc. **POINTS: 2.**

SMART TIP

Experiment with various types of tomatoes such as beefsteak, yellow, and cherry, and different combinations of herbs, such as thyme, tarragon, and cilantro.

TUESDAY	WEDNESDAY	THURSDAY	FRIDAY	SATURDAY
Add chilled, cooked broccoli florets; crumbled feta cheese; and slivered fresh oregano leaves.	Add cooked, chunked potatoes; green beans; flaked canned tuna; a chopped, hard-cooked egg; and a few black olives.	Add cucumber, grape tomatoes, and a few slices of avocado.	Add slivers of pickled beets; chunked, cooked potatoes; and fresh dill sprigs.	Add canned, quartered artichoke hearts; sliced roasted red peppers; halved grape tomatoes; shredded part-skim mozzarella cheese; and chopped peppers or olives.
DRESSING SUGGESTION Olive oil and fresh lemon juice, with a little minced garlic	DRESSING SUGGESTION Creamy light Italian	DRESSING SUGGESTION Light ranch	DRESSING SUGGESTION Equal parts nonfat mayonnaise and nonfat plain yogurt, thinned with water and a dab of horseradish	DRESSING SUGGESTION Garlicky vinaigrette

Cucumber, Black Bean, and Chayote Salad with Spice Tortilla Strips

MAKES 6 SERVINGS

Chayote, a tropical squash, is usually cooked before eating. This exotic vegetable adds crunch and sweetness to salads.

2 (8-inch) flour tortillas, halved and cut into ¼-inch-wide strips
2 teaspoons canola oil
1 teaspoon chili powder
¾ teaspoon salt
¼ teaspoon cayenne
1 chayote, pitted and cut into ½-inch pieces
1 (15½-ounce) can black beans, rinsed and drained
1 cucumber, peeled, seeded, and cut into ½-inch pieces
1 cup cherry tomatoes, halved
½ Haas avocado, cut into ½-inch pieces
3 tablespoons chopped fresh cilantro
3 tablespoons orange juice
2 tablespoons fresh lime juice
1 teaspoon sugar

1. Preheat oven to 400°F. Combine the tortilla strips with 1 teaspoon of the oil, the chili powder, ¼ teaspoon of the salt, and the cayenne in a bowl; toss well to coat. Spread the tortillas in a single layer on a jelly-roll pan and bake until crisp, 5–6 minutes; set aside.

2. Heat a large nonstick skillet over medium-high heat. Swirl in the remaining 1 teaspoon of the oil; add the chayote. Cook until the chayote just starts to soften, 4–5 minutes. Remove from the heat and transfer to a bowl.

3. Add the black beans, cucumber, cherry tomatoes, avocado, cilantro, orange juice, lime juice, sugar, and the remaining ½ teaspoon of the salt to the chayote. Toss the salad with the dressing to coat. Gently stir in the tortilla strips and serve.

Per serving (1 cup): 151 Cal, 6 g Fat, 1 g Sat Fat, 0 mg Chol, 556 mg Sod, 24 g Carb, 5 g Fib, 5 g Prot, 61 mg Calc. **POINTS: 3.**

SMART TIP

You can prepare the Spice Tortilla Strips and chayote several hours ahead and keep at room temperature—then toss the salad with remaining ingredients just before serving.

Three-Bean Salad with Roasted-Garlic Dressing

Most bean salads should be prepared ahead of time; the marinating boosts the flavor.

⅓ cup roasted-garlic vinegar

3 tablespoons olive oil

2 tablespoons chopped fresh parsley

½ teaspoon salt

Freshly ground pepper, to taste

1 (15-ounce) can dark red kidney beans, rinsed and drained

1 (15-ounce) can black-eyed peas, rinsed and drained

1 (15-ounce) can chickpeas (garbanzo beans), rinsed and drained

1 yellow bell pepper, seeded and chopped

½ cup chopped red onion

Combine the vinegar, oil, parsley, salt, and pepper in a large bowl. Add all the beans and chickpeas, the bell pepper, and onion; toss to coat. Cover and refrigerate until chilled, about 2 hours.

Per serving: 187 Cal, 6 g Fat, 1 g Sat Fat, 0 mg Chol, 423 mg Sod, 25 g Carb, 7 g Fib, 9 g Prot, 58 mg Calc. **POINTS: 3.**

SMART TIP

Roasted-garlic vinegar can be found in large supermarkets or specialty-food stores. To make your own, whisk one large clove of mashed roasted garlic into ⅓ cup vinegar.

super bowls

Salade Cote d'Azur

MAKES 4 SERVINGS

This salad is classically French in its use of cooked seasonal vegetables rather than lettuce. It's perfect for making ahead (or for using up leftover cooked veggies). Just prepare and chill the vegetables up to two days in advance, and toss them with the simple dressing immediately before serving.

3   medium or 6 small golden or red beets

½   pound haricots verts (French green beans), trimmed

¼   pound wax beans, trimmed

1   red bell pepper

1   tomato, cut into wedges

12   large black or green olives (¼ cup), pitted and halved

2   tablespoons minced fresh basil

2   tablespoons minced fresh parsley

2   tablespoons sherry vinegar

4   teaspoons extra-virgin olive oil

½   teaspoon salt

Freshly ground pepper, to taste

1. Simmer the beets in enough water to cover until they are just tender enough to pierce with a fork, 20–30 minutes, depending on size. Plunge into a bowl of ice water to stop the cooking. When cool enough to handle, drain, peel, and cut into wedges. Cover and chill at least 2 hours.

2. Bring a large pot of water to a boil. Add the haricots verts and cook just until they are barely tender, about 2 minutes. Plunge into a bowl of ice water to stop the cooking, then drain. Repeat with the wax beans; they will take about 3 minutes to cook. Cover and chill at least 2 hours.

3. Spray the broiler rack with nonstick spray; preheat the broiler. Broil the bell pepper 4 inches from heat, turning frequently with tongs, until the skin is blackened and blistered all over, about 10 minutes.

4. Place the roasted bell pepper in a small bowl, cover with plastic wrap, and let steam for 10 minutes. When cool enough to handle, peel, seed, and thinly slice.

5. Place the haricots verts, wax beans, roasted pepper, tomato, olives, basil, and parsley in a salad bowl. If using golden beets, add them to the salad; if using red beets, place them in a small bowl to prevent their color from "bleeding" onto the rest of the salad. Drizzle the salad (and, if using, the red beets) with the vinegar and oil and sprinkle with the salt and pepper; toss to coat. Add the red beets to the salad just before serving.

Per serving (1½ cups): 115 Cal, 6 g Fat, 1 g Sat Fat, 0 mg Chol, 462 mg Sod, 15 g Carb, 4 g Fib, 3 g Prot, 65 mg Calc. **POINTS: 2.**

SMART TIP

Substitute asparagus for some of the beans, cooked fingerling potatoes for some of the beets, or toss in fresh sweet-corn kernels or lightly cooked zucchini rounds.

Cilantro-Spiked Coleslaw

Preshredded bags of cabbage make this Southwestern-flavored side dish a snap. For additional crunch and color, add an extra shredded carrot (the packaged blends tend to be stingy with their carrots) and a thinly sliced red bell pepper.

½ cup plain nonfat yogurt

½ cup reduced-fat mayonnaise

3 tablespoons chopped fresh cilantro

2 tablespoons cider vinegar

1 tablespoon sugar

½ teaspoon salt

Freshly ground pepper, to taste

1 (16-ounce) bag preshredded coleslaw

1 small onion, finely chopped

1 jalapeño pepper, seeded and finely chopped (wear gloves when handling to prevent irritation)

Combine the yogurt, mayonnaise, cilantro, vinegar, sugar, salt, and pepper in a large bowl. Add the coleslaw, onion, and jalapeño pepper and toss well.

Per serving (1¼ cups): 167 Cal, 10 g Fat, 2 g Sat Fat, 11 mg Chol, 566 mg Sod, 17 g Carb, 3 g Fib, 4 g Prot, 123 mg Calc. **POINTS: 4.**

SMART TIP

For an Asian-flavored coleslaw, substitute an equal amount of shredded Napa cabbage for the preshredded variety and rice vinegar for the cider vinegar. Sprinkle with 1 teaspoon of Asian dark sesame oil and a splash of soy sauce to finish.

Lentil Spinach Soup

MAKES 6 SERVINGS

🔥 Serve this hearty, simple soup with a slice of crusty bread, store-bought Indian flat breads (*rotis*), or naan. All are available at better grocery stores and Indian markets.

5 cups warm water
1 cup brown lentils, sorted and rinsed
1 tablespoon unsalted butter
1 teaspoon cumin seeds
1 large red onion, halved and thinly sliced
5 medium garlic cloves, minced
1 large tomato, diced
2 Thai, cayenne, or serrano chiles, minced (wear gloves when handling to prevent irritation)
1 teaspoon salt
1 (10-ounce) bag triple-washed spinach, rinsed and coarsely chopped

1. Bring 4 cups of the water and the lentils to a boil in a saucepan over medium-high heat; lower the heat and simmer, partially covered, until the lentils are tender, 20–25 minutes.

2. Melt butter in a large nonstick skillet over medium-high heat. Add the cumin seeds and sizzle just until fragrant, 10–15 seconds. Immediately add the onion and garlic and stir-fry until golden brown, 3–4 minutes.

3. Stir in the tomato, chiles, salt, and the remaining 1 cup of water; bring to a boil. Pour the tomato-onion mixture into the saucepan with the lentils. Simmer, covered, stirring occasionally, until the flavors are blended, about 15 minutes. Stir in the spinach just before serving.

Per serving (1 cup): 161 Cal, 3 g Fat, 1 g Sat Fat, 5 mg Chol, 434 mg Sod, 26 g Carb, 10 g Fib, 11 g Prot, 86 mg Calc. **POINTS: 3.**

SMART TIP

Lentils, beans, and peas should be thoroughly rinsed before use. Pick them over, removing any stones, then place the lentils in a large pot and cover them with several inches of water. Stir and let the lentils settle to the bottom. Pour off the water, and with it any impurities, and the lentils are ready to use.

THE HEAT IS ON

True, most soups taste better the day after, but you'll get even tastier results if you follow a few simple rules when reheating:

■ Reheat to a slow simmer (don't recook the soup), and then serve immediately.

■ Taste the soup after reheating and season as needed (flavors can fade in the fridge).

■ Thin bean and grain soups with broth or water when reheating—they can thicken as they stand.

■ Volatile flavors such as wine, vinegar, lemon or lime juice, chiles, and garlic can change in the freezer. Leave them out if you're making a soup that you plan to freeze later, but tape a list of the ingredients you've omitted to the freezer container. After you've thawed and reheated the soup, stir in the ingredients and simmer a few minutes.

Zucchini Basil Soup

MAKES 8 SERVINGS

Try garnishing this vegetarian warm-weather soup with kernels of fresh sweet corn and a few basil leaves.

1 tablespoon extra-virgin olive oil
1 tablespoon unsalted butter
1 large onion, sliced
5 cups water
1 large (8-ounce) potato, peeled and chopped
2 vegetarian vegetable bouillon cubes, crumbled
6 medium zucchini, chopped
4–5 tablespoons chopped fresh basil
Freshly ground pepper, to taste

1. Heat a large saucepan over medium-high heat. Swirl in the oil and the butter, then add the onion. Cook until softened, 5–8 minutes. Add the water, potato, and bouillon cubes; bring to a boil. Reduce the heat and simmer until the potato is tender, about 8 minutes.

2. Add the zucchini; return to a boil and simmer until barely tender, about 5 minutes (do not overcook, as it will dull the soup's bright color). Remove from the heat and let cool slightly.

3. Puree in batches in a food processor until smooth, adding the basil in the final batch. Season with the pepper and serve at once.

Per serving (1¼ cups): 79 Cal, 3 g Fat, 1 g Sat Fat, 4 mg Chol, 223 mg Sod, 11 g Carb, 3 g Fib, 3 g Prot, 34 mg Calc. **POINTS: 1.**

SMART TIP

Although it will no longer be vegetarian, this soup is delicious made with chicken bouillon cubes rather than the vegetable varieties. Or, if you have it on hand, substitute five cups of homemade or reduced-sodium canned vegetable or chicken broth for the water and bouillon cubes. Season the soup with 1 teaspoon salt. For a more textured soup, reserve 1 cup of the chopped zucchini and stir it in after you've pureed the soup.

Pumpkin-Turnip Soup with Cinnamon Croutons

MAKES 4 SERVINGS

Peppery yellow-fleshed turnips and sweet pumpkin are a winning combination. This soup tastes even better reheated the next day.

2 cups fresh or frozen chopped yellow turnips, cooked

1 cup low-sodium chicken broth

1 cup canned pumpkin puree

¼ cup water

¼ teaspoon salt

¼ teaspoon ground ginger

¼ teaspoon cinnamon

⅛ teaspoon ground nutmeg

Dash ground white pepper

1 cup evaporated fat-free milk

4 teaspoons reduced-calorie margarine

¾ teaspoon sugar

2 slices multigrain or whole-wheat bread

Fresh parsley sprigs

1. Combine the turnips, broth, pumpkin, water, salt, ginger, ⅛ teaspoon of the cinnamon, the nutmeg, and pepper in a medium saucepan; whisk in the milk. Heat slowly and bring just to a simmer, stirring occasionally.

2. Meanwhile, combine the margarine, sugar, and the remaining ⅛ teaspoon cinnamon in a small bowl; spread over the bread and cut into small cubes. Toast the bread in a toaster oven or under the broiler until golden brown. Serve the soup garnished with a parsley sprig, with the croutons on the side or sprinkled on top.

Per serving (1¼ cups soup plus croutons): 318 Cal, 5 g Fat, 1 g Sat Fat, 2 mg Chol, 417 mg Sod, 60 g Carb, 7 g Fib, 12 g Prot, 106 mg Calc.
POINTS: 6.

SMART TIP

If you're planning to make the soup a day ahead, prepare the croutons as directed and store at room temperature in an airtight container.

FRUIT SOUP IN A SNAP

Cool, sweet, and refreshing, fruit soups are the essence of summer in a bowl. They're also a perfect snack or starter on a hot summer day—and are ridiculously easy to make. Here's our basic recipe:

1. Start with 1 cup of the juiciest, sweetest, ripest chopped fruits or berries you can find—peaches, cantaloupe, honeydew melon, strawberries, raspberries, or blueberries come to mind—and place them in a blender with ¼ cup of low-fat buttermilk, plain low-fat yogurt, or orange juice.

2. Puree, adding water if needed to reach a substantial soup consistency; you should have about 1 cup of soup.

3. Taste and stir in a little honey if sweetness is needed (1 **POINT** per tablespoon), and season with a sprinkle of ground nutmeg (if using buttermilk or yogurt), fresh lemon juice (if using OJ), grated citrus rind, or some chopped fresh mint. Chill thoroughly.

Matzo Ball Soup

MAKES 8 SERVINGS

Adding seltzer to the matzo ball mixture is the secret to keeping them light and fluffy.

2 large eggs
2 tablespoons canola oil
¼ teaspoon salt
¾ cup matzo meal
3 tablespoons seltzer
4 (14½-ounce) cans reduced-sodium vegetable broth
½ cup fresh flat-leaf parsley leaves
2 tablespoons chopped fresh dill

1. Whisk the eggs, oil, and salt together in a medium bowl. Stir in the matzo meal and seltzer just until smooth. Cover and refrigerate 30 minutes. With wet hands, shape the mixture into sixteen 1-inch balls.

2. Bring 8 cups of water to a rolling boil in a soup pot, then carefully drop in the balls one at a time. Return to a boil, then reduce the heat and simmer, covered, until the matzo balls are soft throughout, 35–40 minutes. Drain matzo balls and set aside.

3. Add the broth to the soup pot and bring to a simmer. Drop in the cooked matzo balls and simmer until heated through, 5 minutes; stir in the parsley and dill just before serving.

Per serving (1 cup broth with 2 matzo balls): 111 Cal, 5 g Fat, 1 g Sat Fat, 53 mg Chol, 327 mg Sod, 14 g Carb, 1 g Fib, 3 g Prot, 0 mg Calc. **POINTS: 2.**

SMART TIP

You can prepare matzo balls one day ahead. Refrigerate them together in a covered container large enough to hold them in a single layer. If you like, you can add steamed carrot coins (1 cup cooked equals 1 *POINT*) to the broth.

super bowls

Chilled Sweet-Cherry Soup

MAKES 1 SERVING

Cold soups make the ideal summer lunch or low-*POINTS* snack, and this one takes advantage of sweet cherries—beauties among summer's bounty. Red-fleshed Bing or golden Rainier cherries will both work nicely in this recipe.

12 large sweet cherries, pitted
½ cup low-fat buttermilk
Pinch ground nutmeg

Combine the cherries and buttermilk in a blender; puree until smooth. Refrigerate, covered, until chilled. Serve, sprinkled with the nutmeg.

Per serving: 105 Cal, 2 g Fat, 1 g Sat Fat, 5 mg Chol, 129 mg Sod, 19 g Carb, 1 g Fib, 5 g Prot, 154 mg Calc. **POINTS: 2.**

SMART TIP

For added flavor and texture, garnish the soup with a sprinkling of Gorgonzola, blue, or feta cheese and walnut pieces (1 tablespoon of either will add 1 *POINT* to your tally).

Green Chile and Turkey Stew

MAKES 4 SERVINGS

Mild-flavored Anaheim chiles are teamed with green and red bell peppers to create complex flavor with a gentle bite. (If you're not lucky enough to find fresh chiles in your market, just substitute a 4-ounce can of whole green chiles, well drained, seeded, and chopped, and skip Step 1.) The stew has a soupy texture, so we like to serve it garnished with toasted corn tortilla strips. Whole-wheat flour tortillas or corn on the cob make a nice accompaniment along with a crisp green salad.

2 Anaheim chiles
1 tablespoon vegetable oil
½ pound skinless boneless turkey breast, cut into ½-inch cubes
1 cup chopped sweet onion
½ red bell pepper, seeded and chopped
½ green bell pepper, seeded and chopped
2 garlic cloves, minced
1 (14½-ounce) can reduced-sodium beef broth
2 medium tomatoes, peeled and chopped
1 teaspoon ground cumin
1 teaspoon dried oregano
½ teaspoon salt

1. Spray the broiler rack with nonstick spray; preheat the broiler. Broil the chiles 4 inches from the heat, turning frequently with tongs, until the skin is shriveled and darkened, 10–20 minutes. Place the chiles in a small bowl, cover with plastic wrap, and steam 10-20 minutes. When cool enough to handle, peel, seed, and cut into 1-inch pieces (wear gloves when handling to prevent irritation).

2. Heat a large nonstick skillet over medium-high heat. Swirl in the oil, then add the turkey. Cook until browned, 5–8 minutes. Transfer to a plate.

3. Add the onion, the red and green bell peppers, and the garlic; cook until the onion is softened, about 8 minutes. Return the turkey and its juices to the skillet and add the broth, chiles, tomatoes, cumin, oregano, and salt. Simmer, stirring occasionally, until thickened, about 30 minutes.

Per serving (1 cup): 181 Cal, 6 g Fat, 1 g Sat Fat, 44 mg Chol, 411 mg Sod, 11 g Carb, 2 g Fib, 20 g Prot, 41 mg Calc. **POINTS: 4.**

SMART TIP

To toast corn tortilla strips for a garnish, just slice two (6-inch) corn tortillas into ¼-inch-wide strips. Spray a large nonstick skillet with nonstick spray, then add the tortilla strips and sauté until lightly crisped and fragrant, about 2 minutes. Sprinkle over the stew just before serving (add 1 *POINT* per serving).

Chicken and Swiss Chard Stew with Fennel

MAKES 4 SERVINGS

Hearty Italian stews are often flavored with fennel-rich sausage and earthy Swiss chard. You'll need to use only the leaves of the chard, but don't throw away the stems—chop them finely and add them to soups or stews, or sauté them with onion and stir in some beaten eggs to make a delicious frittata.

2 bunches (about 3 pounds) Swiss chard, cleaned, stems trimmed

4 (5-ounce) skinless boneless chicken breast halves

1 tablespoon crushed fennel seeds

¾ teaspoon salt

2 teaspoons olive oil

1 large garlic clove, minced

2 plum tomatoes, chopped

¼ teaspoon crushed red pepper

1 cup reduced-sodium chicken broth

1 cup canned navy or great Northern beans, rinsed and drained

1. Place the chard, with water still clinging to the leaves, in a large pot or Dutch oven. Cook over medium-high heat, stirring once, until deflated and softened, 6–8 minutes. Set aside.

2. Sprinkle both sides of the chicken with the fennel seeds, pressing them into the meat with your fingers to help them adhere; sprinkle with ½ teaspoon of the salt.

3. Heat a large nonstick skillet over medium-high heat. Swirl in 1 teaspoon of the oil, then add the chicken. Cook, turning once, until browned, 2–3 minutes per side. Transfer to a plate and keep warm.

4. Add the remaining 1 teaspoon of the oil and the garlic to the skillet; cook until fragrant, about 30 seconds. Add the tomatoes and crushed red pepper, and cook until softened, 3–4 minutes. Add the chard with ⅓ cup of its cooking liquid (discard the remaining liquid), the broth, beans, and the remaining ¼ teaspoon salt. Bring to a boil; return the chicken to the skillet and submerge it in the chard. Reduce the heat to low and simmer (do not boil), covered, until the chicken is cooked through, 8–9 minutes.

Per serving (1 breast half with about 1 cup chard mixture): 324 Cal, 7 g Fat, 2 g Sat Fat, 77 mg Chol, 1198 mg Sod, 25 g Carb, 9 g Fib, 41 g Prot, 214 mg Calc. **POINTS: 6.**

SMART TIP

When simmering the chicken at the end of Step 3, keep the liquid around the chicken at a high simmer—with small bubbles occasionally appearing—but not boiling, since a true boil will toughen the meat. If you prefer, you can keep the mixture at a low simmer, with an occasional lazy bubble breaking the surface. Just cook it about 5 minutes longer than the recipe specifies.

Spring Stew

MAKES 4 SERVINGS

Enjoy this savory, light stew with a hunk of crusty whole-grain bread and a crisp salad. Try not to overcook the chicken; the cubes are not fully cooked when they are browned but will cook through quickly once you add them to the stew.

4 (5-ounce) skinless boneless chicken breast halves, cubed
½ teaspoon salt
Freshly ground pepper, to taste
2 teaspoons olive oil
1 large shallot, finely chopped
¼ cup dry white wine
1¼ cups reduced-sodium chicken broth
1 pound small red potatoes, halved
1 medium carrot, thinly sliced
½ teaspoon minced fresh thyme, or ¼ teaspoon dried
½ teaspoon minced fresh rosemary, or ¼ teaspoon dried
1 teaspoon all-purpose flour

1. Sprinkle the chicken all over with the salt and pepper. Heat a large nonstick skillet over high heat. Swirl in 1 teaspoon of the oil, then add the chicken and cook, turning once, until browned, 2–3 minutes per side. Transfer the chicken to a plate; reduce the heat slightly.

2. Add the remaining 1 teaspoon oil and the shallot; cook 1 minute. Add the wine; cook, scraping up the browned bits from the bottom of the skillet, about 30 seconds. Stir in 1 cup of the broth, the potatoes, carrot, thyme, and rosemary; bring to a boil. Reduce the heat and cook at a low boil, stirring occasionally, until the potatoes are tender, 12–15 minutes.

3. Whisk the flour into the remaining ¼ cup broth in a small bowl. Stir into the stew; add the chicken and continue cooking until the chicken is cooked through, 1–3 minutes more.

Per serving (about 1½ cups): 310 Cal, 7 g Fat, 2 g Sat Fat, 77 mg Chol, 526 mg Sod, 26 g Carb, 3 g Fib, 34 g Prot, 41 mg Calc. **POINTS: 6.**

SMART TIP

This recipe also works nicely with pork instead of chicken. Use a 1¼-pound pork tenderloin or four thin-cut, 5-ounce boneless pork chops. Trim off as much visible fat as you can before you cut the pork into chunks; it will take slightly longer to cook through in Step 3. The pork is done when a piece is barely pink in the center.

super bowls

Boeuf Bourguignon

MAKES 8 SERVINGS

Boeuf Bourguignon, or beef Burgundy-style, is a French classic. Traditionally, the onions, mushrooms, and beef are browned in pork fat. We've used olive oil instead and added small red potatoes to round out a wonderful one-pot recipe.

1¼ cups dry red wine

1 tablespoon + 1 teaspoon extra-virgin olive oil

2 teaspoons chopped fresh thyme

½ teaspoon kosher salt

Freshly ground pepper, to taste

2 pounds stewing beef, trimmed of all visible fat and cut into 2-inch squares, ½-inch thick

1 (10-ounce) package pearl onions, peeled

1 (10-ounce) package small white mushrooms, washed and trimmed

2 tablespoons all-purpose flour

1 tablespoon tomato paste

1 (14½-ounce) can reduced-sodium beef broth

1 garlic clove, minced

½ bay leaf

1 pound small Red Bliss potatoes, or 1 pound red potatoes, cut into bite-size pieces

½ cup water

1. Combine ¼ cup of the wine, 1 teaspoon of the oil, 1 teaspoon of the thyme, and the salt and pepper in a zip-close plastic bag; add the beef. Squeeze out the air and seal the bag; turn to coat the beef. Refrigerate 1 hour, turning occasionally. Drain and discard the marinade; pat the beef dry with a paper towel.

2. Preheat the oven to 400°F. Place a large cast-iron skillet in the oven and heat 10 minutes.

3. Add the remaining 1 tablespoon oil and the onions to the hot skillet, stirring to coat the onions. Bake until the onions begin to color, about 10 minutes, shaking the pan occasionally. Add the mushrooms, stirring to coat. Bake 5 minutes more, stirring twice. Transfer onions and mushrooms to a medium bowl; set aside.

4. Return the skillet to the oven and heat 5 minutes. Add the beef to the skillet in a single layer; bake 5 minutes. Turn the beef and bake 5 minutes more. Stir in the flour and tomato paste. Bake 10 minutes more, stirring once. Add the remaining 1 cup wine, the broth, the remaining 1 teaspoon of the thyme, the garlic, and bay leaf. Stir, cover the skillet tightly, reduce the heat to 350°F, and bake 1 hour. Add the potatoes and the water, cover, and cook 30 minutes. Stir in the mushrooms, onions, and their juices; cook until the beef is just tender, about 15 minutes more. Discard the bay leaf.

Per serving (1 cup): 274 Cal, 10 g Fat, 3 g Fat, 51 mg Chol, 165 mg Sod, 18 g Carb, 2 g Fib, 27 g Prot, 25 mg Calc. **POINTS: 6.**

SMART TIP

The technique used here is braising, a combination of two cooking methods; first, dry heat is used to brown the meat, then moist heat finishes cooking the meat slowly. It's worth the time: Browning adds incomparable flavor, and slow-cooking makes the meat meltingly tender.

weight watchers

Seafood Gumbo

MAKES 4 SERVINGS

Gumbo, an African contribution to Louisiana cookery, is a spicy cross between a soup and a stew. There are many variations of ingredients, but all gumbos begin with dark roux, a combination of flour and fat, slowly browned. As old Creole cooks used to say, "Don't hurry the roux. You'll spoil your gumbo."

½ pound okra, thinly sliced

1 large onion, thinly sliced

1 green bell pepper, seeded and sliced

2 celery stalks, sliced

2 garlic cloves, crushed

2 tablespoons olive oil

2 tablespoons all-purpose flour

3 cups water

2 bay leaves

1 teaspoon dried thyme

½ teaspoon cayenne

½ cup canned diced tomatoes, drained

½ pound large shrimp, peeled and deveined

½ pound lump crabmeat, picked over

¼ teaspoon salt

Freshly ground pepper, to taste

1. Spray a large nonstick skillet with nonstick spray and set over medium-high heat. Add the okra, onion, bell pepper, celery, and garlic. Cook until softened, 5 minutes. Transfer the vegetables to a bowl and set aside.

2. To make the roux, add the oil to the skillet and then the flour; stir until well-blended. Cook, stirring, until the flour is a rich brown color but not black, about 10 minutes.

3. Add the water in a thin stream, stirring continuously to remove any lumps, and bring to a simmer. Stir in the bay leaves, thyme, and cayenne; then add the tomatoes. Return the vegetables to the pan and simmer 5 minutes. Add the shrimp and crabmeat and simmer just until the shrimp are opaque in the center, 2–3 minutes. Discard the bay leaves. Season with the salt and pepper.

Per serving (2 cups): 236 Cal, 9 g Fat, 1 g Sat Fat, 127 mg Chol, 515 mg Sod, 16 g Carb, 4 g Fib, 24 g Prot, 159 mg Calc. **POINTS: 5.**

SMART TIP

This version of gumbo includes okra, which produces a thickening agent when cooked. Other recipes can use filé powder—ground, dried sassafras leaves.

Portuguese Fisherman's Stew

MAKES 4 SERVINGS

Portuguese immigrants of the early 1800s, renowned as navigators and fishermen, chose to settle in the fishing communities of Rhode Island, Massachusetts, and the Connecticut coasts. This dish combines an array of seafood with the signature Portuguese flavorings of linguiça, a garlicky Portuguese sausage, and saffron.

2 red potatoes, cut into eighths
1 medium carrot, peeled and chopped
½ onion, chopped
2 ounces linguiça, chorizo, or reduced-fat kielbasa, sliced
2 garlic cloves, minced
½ pound tomatoes, chopped
1 (8-ounce) bottle clam juice
½ cup dry white wine
½ teaspoon saffron threads, crushed
¼ teaspoon dried oregano
¼ teaspoon crushed red pepper
8 littleneck clams, scrubbed
8 mussels, scrubbed and debearded
¼ pound medium shrimp, peeled and deveined
¼ pound cod fillet
¼ pound sea scallops
1 tablespoon chopped fresh cilantro

1. Spray an 8-quart saucepan with nonstick spray and set over medium heat. Add the potatoes, carrot, onion, linguiça, and garlic; cook until the onion begins to soften, about 6 minutes. Stir in the tomatoes, clam juice, wine, saffron, oregano, and crushed red pepper; bring to a boil. Cover, reduce the heat, and simmer 15 minutes. Add the clams and simmer, covered, 6 minutes.
2. Stir in the mussels, cover, and simmer 3 minutes more. Add the shrimp, cod, and scallops; cook until the shrimp are pink and no longer opaque, about 5 minutes. Discard any clams and mussels that have not opened. Stir in the cilantro and serve.

Per serving (2 cups): 277 Cal, 7 g Fat, 2 g Sat Fat, 84 mg Chol, 501 mg Sod, 25 g Carb, 3 g Fib, 26 g Prot, 75 mg Calc. **POINTS: 6.**

SMART TIP

Look for linguiça (lin-GWEE-sa) in Spanish and American markets.

California Cioppino

MAKES 8 SERVINGS

Cioppino, pronounced "cha-PEE-no," is a traditional fish stew from the San Francisco Bay area. One of the important ingredients is Dungeness crab, which is available in the winter months on the California coast. We replaced it with easier-to-find lump crabmeat, but by all means, use Dungeness crab if it's available. You can also use king crab legs cut into chunks, or canned crabmeat.

- 1 tablespoon extra-virgin olive oil
- 1 Spanish onion, finely chopped
- 2 large garlic cloves, minced
- 1 cup dry red wine
- 2 (8-ounce) bottles clam juice
- 1 pound mussels, scrubbed
- 1 (28-ounce) can crushed tomatoes in tomato puree
- 1 teaspoon Italian seasoning
- ¼ teaspoon kosher salt

Freshly ground pepper, to taste

- ½ pound halibut fillet, cut into chunks
- ½ pound medium shrimp, peeled and deveined
- ½ pound lump crabmeat

1. Heat a large nonstick skillet over medium-high heat. Swirl in the oil, then add the onion. Cook until softened, 5–6 minutes. Add the garlic and cook until fragrant. Add the wine and simmer until the liquid is reduced by half, about 5 minutes. Add the clam juice and bring to a boil. Add the mussels, cover, and cook until they open. Transfer the mussels to a bowl, discarding any that do not open. Discard the top shell of each mussel and refrigerate the mussels.

2. Add the tomatoes, Italian seasoning, salt, and pepper to the skillet. Bring to a boil; reduce the heat to low and simmer until the stew begins to thicken, stirring occasionally. Add the halibut and shrimp; cook, stirring gently, until fish is opaque and shrimp turn pink. Remove from the heat; top with the crabmeat and mussels. Cover and let stand 10 minutes to warm through and blend the flavors.

Per serving (1½ cups): 164 Cal, 4 g Fat, 1 g Sat Fat, 73 mg Chol, 651 mg Sod, 9 g Carb, 1 g Fib, 22 g Prot, 69 mg Calc. **POINTS: 3.**

SMART TIP

Like any good fish recipe, this one accepts many substitutions, depending on what looks fresh in the market. If mussels are not available, substitute small clams. If you can't find halibut, use another mild-flavored, moderately firm-fleshed fish, such as cod, grouper, snapper, or catfish.

5-**POINT** WONDERS

Believe it—"stick to your ribs" dishes
don't have to "stick to your thighs!"
To prove our point (and fill your plate),
each of these fabulous entrées contains
only **5 POINTS** or less.

Wild Mushroom Frittata

MAKES 4 SERVINGS

Use any assortment of mushrooms to add wonderful flavor to the frittata, which makes a fast-and-tasty dinner when served with a mixed green salad.

2 large eggs
6 egg whites
2 tablespoons water
¼ teaspoon salt
Freshly ground pepper, to taste
1 tablespoon olive oil
¾ pound assorted mushrooms (such as cremini, portobello, and shiitake), coarsely chopped
1 shallot, thinly sliced
½ teaspoon dried oregano
¼ cup shredded part-skim mozzarella cheese
1 tablespoon grated Parmesan cheese
1 tablespoon chopped fresh basil

1. Beat the eggs, egg whites, water, salt, and pepper in a bowl until frothy.

2. Heat a medium nonstick skillet with an ovenproof handle over medium-high heat. Swirl in the oil, then add the mushrooms, shallot, and oregano. Cook until the mushrooms are golden, about 5 minutes. Add the egg mixture to the mushrooms, stirring gently to combine. Reduce the heat and cook, without stirring, until the eggs are set, 12–15 minutes.

3. Preheat the broiler, then sprinkle the frittata with the mozzarella. Broil the frittata, 5 inches from heat, until the top is lightly browned, about 2 minutes. Allow to stand 5 minutes before serving. Sprinkle with the Parmesan and basil and cut into 4 wedges.

Per serving (¼ of frittata): 156 Cal, 7 g Fat, 2 g Sat Fat, 110 mg Chol, 334 mg Sod, 9 g Carb, 2 g Fib, 14 g Prot, 103 mg Calc. **POINTS: 3.**

SMART TIP

Wild mushrooms have a wonderful woodsy flavor, but they can be expensive. If you're watching your budget, use a combination of half white and half wild mushrooms instead.

Stir-fried Beef with Vegetables

MAKES 4 SERVINGS

Substitute boneless skinless chicken breasts for the steak, if desired.

2 tablespoons reduced-sodium soy sauce

1 tablespoon dry sherry or rice wine

¾ pound lean round steak, trimmed and thinly sliced

1 (1-pound) bunch asparagus, trimmed and cut into 1½-inch lengths

3 large carrots, thinly sliced

2 tablespoons water

1 teaspoon Asian sesame oil

1 teaspoon cornstarch

½ teaspoon sugar

Freshly ground black pepper, to taste

3 teaspoons peanut oil

4 scallions, minced (white and green parts)

2 large garlic cloves, minced

1 tablespoon minced peeled fresh ginger

1 tablespoon fermented black beans, rinsed and chopped

1. Combine 1 tablespoon of the soy sauce and the sherry in a zip-close plastic bag; add the steak. Squeeze out the air and seal the bag; turn to coat the steak. Refrigerate 10 minutes.

2. Meanwhile, bring 1 inch of water to a boil in a large, heavy nonstick skillet. Add the asparagus and carrots; cover and simmer until barely crisp-tender, about 5 minutes. Drain in a colander under cold water to stop the cooking; set aside.

3. To prepare the flavoring sauce, whisk together the water, the remaining 1 tablespoon soy sauce, the sesame oil, cornstarch, sugar, and pepper in a small bowl; set aside.

4. Wipe out the skillet and return it to the heat; let it get very hot. Swirl in 2 teaspoons of the peanut oil. When the oil is just beginning to shimmer, add the beef. Stir-fry until browned on the edges but still pink in the center, about 2 minutes. Transfer the beef and pan juices to a heatproof bowl and keep warm.

5. Return the skillet to the heat; let it get very hot. Swirl in the remaining 1 teaspoon of peanut oil. When the oil shimmers, add the scallions, garlic, ginger, and black beans. Stir-fry until fragrant, 30 seconds. Add the reserved cooked vegetables and stir-fry until tender, about 6 minutes. Stir in the beef and its juices, then the flavoring sauce. Stir-fry until heated through, 2–3 minutes more. Serve immediately.

Per serving (1¼ cups): 210 Cal, 8 g Fat, 2 g Sat Fat, 45 mg Chol, 292 mg Sod, 16 g Carb, 4 g Fib, 20 g Prot, 56 mg Calc. **POINTS: 4.**

SMART TIP

Add 2 cups of shredded spinach or chopped watercress at the end of cooking, when you return the beef to the skillet. The greens create a lot of liquid, so use only 1 tablespoon of water when you prepare the sauce.

Turkey Burgers

MAKES 4 SERVINGS

A classic family staple, burgers are ideal fare for busy cooks with hungry families.

1 pound ground skinless turkey

½ red onion, chopped

1 large egg, beaten

2 tablespoons chopped fresh parsley

1 garlic clove, minced

½ teaspoon dried tarragon

½ teaspoon salt

¼ teaspoon freshly ground pepper

1. Preheat the broiler. Spray the broiler rack with nonstick cooking spray.

2. Lightly combine the turkey, onion, egg, parsley, garlic, tarragon, salt, and pepper in a bowl. Form into 4 burgers. Broil 4 inches from heat until brown, about 5 minutes on each side.

Per serving (1 burger): 169 Cal, 10 g Fat, 3 g Sat Fat, 121 mg Chol, 390 mg Sod, 2 g Carb, 0 g Fib, 17 g Prot, 32 mg Calc. **POINTS: 4.**

SMART TIP

This is delicious with a side of baked "fries", but if you're in a hurry, whip up a quick coleslaw while the burgers cook.

LEAN, LOW-*POINTS* TOPPERS

Sure, burgers are certainly all-American, but why not celebrate the burger by trying an assortment of international-style toppings that all have one thing in common: big flavor.

TOPPING
All-American: 1 slice fat-free American cheese
German: Red-cabbage slaw and thinly sliced cucumber tossed with vinegar
Greek: 6 chopped olives and tomato slices sprinkled with minced fresh oregano
Italian: ¼ cup fat-free shredded mozzarella, 1 chopped plum tomato, and chopped fresh basil
Japanese: Low-sodium teriyaki sauce and wasabi mustard
Mexican: ¼ avocado, chopped; prepared salsa; and pickled sliced jalapeños.

Pot au Feu

MAKES 8 SERVINGS

Pot au feu (poh-toh-FEUH)—"pot in the fire"—usually includes beef, poultry, pork, and an assortment of vegetables simmered in a flavorful broth. This dish is naturally low in fat. Serve it with boiled Yukon gold potatoes. If you like, stir in a dab of Dijon mustard or grated horseradish to round out the flavors of this dish.

2 pounds beef rump roast, trimmed of all visible fat and tied with string

2 (14½-ounce) cans reduced-sodium beef broth

2 (14½-ounce) cans reduced-sodium chicken broth

4 cups water

½ bay leaf

¼ teaspoon dried thyme

¼ teaspoon kosher salt

Freshly ground pepper, to taste

4 leeks, split lengthwise and cleaned

4 carrots, peeled and cut into 2-inch pieces

1 celery heart, trimmed and cut lengthwise into 8 wedges

2 turnips, peeled and cut into quarters

½ small green cabbage, trimmed and cut into 8 wedges

2 tablespoons chopped fresh parsley

1. Combine the beef, the beef and chicken broths, and the water in a large, heavy pot or Dutch oven; bring to a boil over medium-high heat. Skim any foam that rises to the surface, reduce the heat to medium, and add the bay leaf, thyme, salt, and pepper. Leaving the lid slightly ajar, gently simmer the beef until almost tender, about 2½ hours. With tongs, transfer the beef to a plate.

2. Add the leeks, carrots, celery heart, turnips, and cabbage to the broth, then top with the reserved beef. Cover and simmer until the vegetables and beef are tender, about 30 minutes. Remove from the heat and let stand 20–30 minutes to blend the flavors.

3. To serve, transfer the beef to a cutting board and remove the string. Slice ¼-inch thick and arrange the slices on a platter. Arrange the vegetables around the beef and moisten with some of the broth; sprinkle with the parsley. Serve in shallow bowls, ladling extra broth over the beef and vegetables.

Per serving (2½ cups): 198 Cal, 4 g Fat, 1 g Sat Fat, 43 mg Chol, 503 mg Sod, 17 g Carb, 5 g Fib, 25 g Prot, 107 mg Calc. **POINTS: 3.**

SMART TIP

To clean leeks, trim the roots, leaving the root ends intact to hold the layers together. Slice them lengthwise, fan open the layers, and swish them in a large bowl of cool water. Let stand a few minutes to allow the grit to fall to the bottom, then lift them out.

Chicken Cacciatore

MAKES 6 SERVINGS

Cacciatore is the Italian word for hunter or woodsman. The dish traditionally includes mushrooms and a variety of herbs and tomatoes, cooked into a flavorful sauce. Serve it over quick-cooking polenta—or with a green salad for a lighter meal.

1 (3½-pound) chicken, skinned and cut into 8 pieces, wings discarded
½ teaspoon Italian seasoning
½ teaspoon kosher salt
Freshly ground pepper, to taste
1 shallot, minced
1 garlic clove, minced
4 cups cremini mushrooms (about ½ pound), sliced
⅓ cup dry white wine
1 (14½-ounce) can diced tomatoes in juice
1 cup reduced-sodium chicken broth
½ bay leaf
2 tablespoons chopped fresh flat-leaf parsley

1. Rinse the chicken pieces and pat dry with paper towels. Cut both breast pieces in half.

2. Combine the Italian seasoning, salt, and pepper in a small bowl. Sprinkle the mixture on both sides of the chicken pieces. Let stand at room temperature 10 minutes.

3. Preheat the oven to 400°F. Spray an ovenproof skillet with nonstick spray and set over medium-high heat. Add half of the chicken and cook until browned on all sides, 7–8 minutes. Transfer to a plate; repeat with the remaining chicken.

4. Spray the skillet with nonstick spray and set over low heat. Add the shallot and garlic; cook until fragrant. Stir in the mushrooms; cook, stirring, until they begin to release their juices, 7–8 minutes. Raise the heat to high, add the wine, and bring to a simmer. Cook, stirring occasionally, 3–4 minutes. Add the tomatoes, broth, and the bay leaf, bring to a boil, and cook 10 minutes more, stirring occasionally.

5. Return the chicken to the skillet, submerge it in the sauce, and bring to a gentle boil. Place the skillet in the oven and bake until the chicken is cooked through, 45–50 minutes. Discard the bay leaf and sprinkle with the parsley.

Per serving (1½ cups): 170 Cal, 4 g Fat, 1 Sat Fat, 79 mg Chol, 563 mg Sod, 5 g Carb, 1 g Fib, 27 g Prot, 24 mg Calc. **POINTS: 4.**

SMART TIP

Cooking chicken on the bone keeps it moist and adds flavor as well. Save the chicken wings to make chicken stock. Keep a resealable bag of wings, necks, and backs in the freezer. When you have a few pounds, you can make your own chicken stock. For a thicker sauce, transfer the cooked chicken pieces to a platter and simmer the sauce, uncovered, until thickened, 8–10 minutes.

Coq au Vin

MAKES 6 SERVINGS

Coq au Vin is a classic dish that originated in France. A close relative to Boeuf Bourguignon (page 47), this dish can also be prepared with white wine. If you can't find small mushrooms, cut larger ones in halves or quarters.

1 (3½-pound) chicken, skinned and cut into 8 pieces, wings discarded
½ teaspoon kosher salt
Freshly ground pepper, to taste
1 bacon slice, cut into ½-inch strips
1 onion, chopped
3 tablespoons all-purpose flour
1 (14½-ounce) can reduced-sodium chicken broth
1 cup dry red wine
1 (10-ounce) package small mushrooms, washed and trimmed
½ pound baby carrots
½ bay leaf
¼ teaspoon dried thyme

1. Preheat the oven to 375°F. Rinse the chicken pieces and pat dry with paper towels. Cut both breast pieces in half. Sprinkle the chicken pieces all over with the salt and pepper.
2. Heat a large nonstick skillet over medium-high heat. Add the bacon. Cook until crisp; transfer to a bowl. Add the chicken pieces to the skillet and cook until golden brown on all sides, 7–8 minutes. Transfer the chicken pieces to a plate.
3. Add the onion to the skillet; cook until softened, 5–6 minutes. Sprinkle with the flour and cook, stirring, until golden brown, about 10 minutes. Add the broth and wine; bring just to a boil, stirring constantly, and simmer until slightly thickened. Add the browned chicken, the mushrooms, baby carrots, bacon, bay leaf, and thyme. Bring to a boil, cover and bake until the chicken is cooked through, 30 minutes. Discard the bay leaf.

Per serving (2½ cups): 235 Cal, 8 g Fat, 2 g Sat Fat, 84 mg Chol, 407 mg Sod, 11 g Carb, 2 g Fib, 28 g Prot, 39 mg Calc. **POINTS: 5.**

SMART TIP

This dish can be prepared a day ahead and reheated in a 350°F oven 20–30 minutes, or until the sauce is bubbling and the chicken is heated through.

Chicken with Radish-Corn Salad

MAKES 4 SERVINGS

Tired of tough, dry chicken? Try this skillet-to-oven method, which practically guarantees the chicken will remain juicy. The short browning time sears the outside, while baking at a moderate temperature keeps the meat moist and prevents the outside from becoming too tough. Use fresh corn in the salad for the best taste, though frozen corn will work, too. For a chilled salad, prepare the recipe through Step 3, omitting the basil. Cover and refrigerate up to two hours ahead; stir in the basil just before serving.

2 cups fresh (from 4 medium ears) or thawed frozen corn kernels

2 cups thinly sliced radishes

1½ cups peeled and diced hothouse cucumber

¼ cup rice vinegar

1¼ teaspoons sugar

¾ teaspoon salt

1 tablespoon thinly sliced fresh basil

Freshly ground pepper, to taste

4 (5-ounce) skinless boneless chicken breast halves

1 teaspoon olive oil

1. Preheat the oven to 350°F. Spray a large nonstick skillet with nonstick spray and set over high heat. Add the corn and cook until charred in spots, 1–2 minutes. Remove from the heat and let cool.

2. Combine the corn, radishes, cucumber, vinegar, sugar, and ¼ teaspoon of the salt in a medium bowl. Stir in the basil and pepper.

3. Sprinkle the chicken all over with the remaining ½ teaspoon salt and the pepper.

4. Return the skillet to medium-high heat. Swirl in the oil. Add the chicken and cook, turning once, until browned, 2–3 minutes per side. Transfer the skillet to the oven and bake until the chicken is cooked through, 8–9 minutes. Serve with the salad.

Per serving (1 breast half with 1 cup salad): 262 Cal, 6 g Fat, 1 g Sat Fat, 77 mg Chol, 526 mg Sod, 21 g Carb, 3 g Fib, 33 g Prot, 41 mg Calc. **POINTS: 5.**

SMART TIP

Hothouse cucumbers, sometimes called English cucumbers, are longer and thinner than regular cucumbers, and you'll usually find them wrapped in plastic. They cost a little more, but because they have thin skin and fewer seeds, they're worth the steeper price. You can use regular cucumbers in this recipe, too, but they should be seeded first: Cut the peeled cucumber in half lengthwise, then scoop out the seeds with a small spoon.

Peruvian-Style Chicken Breasts

MAKES 6 SERVINGS

In Nuevo Latino cuisine, marinades are used to intensify the flavors of chicken. A marinade is a seasoned liquid—usually citrus juice or vinegar—combined with herbs and spices. Chicken is soaked in the marinade to both tenderize and absorb flavor.

¼ cup dry white wine
2 garlic cloves, peeled
2 tablespoons soy sauce
2 tablespoons fresh lime juice
1 tablespoon olive oil
1 canned chipotle en adobo
2 teaspoons honey
2 teaspoons fresh thyme
2 teaspoons paprika
6 (8-ounce) bone-in chicken breasts, skinned
¼ teaspoon salt

1. Combine the wine, garlic, soy sauce, lime juice, olive oil, chipotle, honey, thyme, and paprika in a blender; pulse on high speed until the mixture is smooth, about 2 minutes. Pour the marinade into a zip-close plastic bag; add the chicken. Squeeze out the air and seal the bag; turn to coat the chicken. Refrigerate, turning the bag occasionally, 45 minutes.
2. Meanwhile, preheat the oven to 375°F; lightly spray a jelly-roll pan with nonstick spray.
3. Remove the chicken from the bag, discard the marinade, and arrange the chicken in the pan. Sprinkle chicken with the salt, then roast, basting with the pan juices every 10 minutes, until cooked through, about 45 minutes. Remove chicken from the oven and brush with the pan juices.

Per serving (1 breast): 193 Cal, 5 g Fat, 1 g Sat Fat, 92 mg Chol, 312 mg Sod, 1 g Carb, 0 g Fib, 34 g Prot, 18 mg Calc. **POINTS: 4.**

SMART TIP

A bed of warm greens and a serving of saffron rice with black beans or peas make the perfect foil to this dish.

CUTTING UP A CHICKEN

Clueless when a recipe specifies, "one chicken, cut into 8 pieces?" Here's an easy way to do it.

1. Remove the legs: Pull each leg out away from the body, cutting through the loose skin. Pull up on the leg until the thighbone pops out of its socket and slice through the joint. Slice through the skin, cutting around the thigh, being careful to include the tender "oyster"—the nugget behind the thigh joint.
2. Separate the thighs from the drumsticks: Find the joint connecting each leg to the thigh and cut through it.
3. Remove the wings: Pull on each wing to loosen it from its socket, and then cut through the joint and detach.
4. Separate the breast from the back: Cut through the rib bones on either side of the backbone with poultry shears, staying as close as possible to the backbone.
5. Separate the breast halves: Remove the wishbone from the neck end of the breast, scraping it free with the tip of a sharp knife. Then, skin-side down, cut the breast down the middle, through the breastbone. You should now have eight pieces: two legs, two thighs, two wings, and two breast halves.

Poblano Posole with Grilled Chicken

Posole with hominy is an original New Mexican comfort food that holds a revered position similar to the one that the chili enjoys in Texas. It is a feast-day dish for Mexicans, so you'll find it on many tables at Christmas and New Year's.

6 poblano chiles
¾ pound skinless boneless chicken breasts
1 tablespoon vegetable oil
1 large white onion, finely chopped
3 garlic cloves, minced
2 teaspoons cumin seed, coarsely ground, or ground cumin
1 teaspoon dried oregano
6 cups low-sodium chicken broth
1 (19-ounce) can posole or hominy
½ teaspoon salt
Freshly ground pepper, to taste
1 tablespoon fresh lime juice
8 thin lime slices
Thinly sliced scallions, radishes, and fresh cilantro leaves

1. To prepare the poblanos, spray the broiler rack with nonstick spray and preheat the broiler. Broil chiles 4 inches from heat, turning frequently with tongs, until skin is shriveled and dark, 10–20 minutes. Place chiles in a bowl, cover with plastic wrap, and steam 10 minutes. When cool enough to handle, peel, seed, and chop (wear gloves when handling to prevent irritation).

2. Spray a nonstick ridged grill pan with nonstick spray and heat over medium heat. Grill the chicken, turning once, until cooked through, 5–6 minutes on each side. Transfer to a cutting board and let cool. When cool enough to handle, finely shred the chicken with your fingers. Set aside.

3. Heat a Dutch oven over medium-high heat. Swirl in the oil, then add the onion. Cook until softened. Stir in the garlic, cumin, and oregano and cook until fragrant. Stir in the broth, posole or hominy, chiles, salt, and pepper and cook at a low boil, stirring occasionally, until reduced slightly, about 30 minutes.

4. Add the chicken and lime juice to the posole and heat through, about 3 minutes. Top with the lime slices, scallions, radishes, and cilantro leaves.

Per serving (1 cup): 180 Cal, 5 g Fat, 1 g Sat Fat, 31 mg Chol, 421 mg Sod, 19 g Carb, 3 g Fib, 15 g Prot, 47 mg Calc. **POINTS: 3.**

63

weight watchers

Chinese Chicken and Cabbage Salad

MAKES 4 SERVINGS

Poaching the chicken breast in an aromatic broth builds a wonderful layer of flavor in this colorful salad. Don't throw out the poaching liquid—it makes a virtually **POINTS**-free broth that's ideal for snacking. Store, covered, in the refrigerator for up to five days.

3 (5-ounce) skinless boneless chicken breast halves
1 cup reduced-sodium chicken broth
1 cup water
1 star anise
5 whole black peppercorns
1 quarter-size slice fresh ginger
3 tablespoons fresh lime juice
2 tablespoons rice vinegar
1 jalapeño pepper, seeded and minced (wear gloves when handling to prevent irritation)
1 tablespoon reduced-sodium soy sauce
2 garlic cloves, minced
2 teaspoons sugar
2 teaspoons minced peeled fresh ginger
1 medium head (about 1 pound) Napa cabbage, very thinly sliced
1/3 onion, very thinly sliced
1 yellow bell pepper, seeded and cut into thin strips

1. Combine the chicken, broth, water, star anise, peppercorns, and ginger slice in a medium saucepan. Bring to a boil, then reduce the heat, cover, and simmer until the chicken is nearly cooked through, about 7 minutes. Remove from the heat and let stand, covered, 7 minutes more. Drain the chicken, reserving the liquid for another use. When the chicken is cool enough to handle, shred into bite-size strips.

2. Meanwhile, whisk together the lime juice, vinegar, jalapeño pepper, soy sauce, garlic, sugar, and minced ginger in a large bowl; add the cabbage, onion, and bell pepper and toss. Add the chicken and toss again. Serve immediately, or cover and chill up to 2 hours ahead.

Per serving (2 cups): 172 Cal, 3 g Fat, 1 g Sat Fat, 58 mg Chol, 303 mg Sod, 10 g Carb, 2 g Fib, 26 g Prot, 131 mg Calc. **POINTS: 3.**

SMART TIP

Star anise is a fragrant spice used frequently in Chinese cooking. The pretty eight-pointed "stars" look like wooden flowers, and their licoricelike, slightly piney flavor is incomparable. Look for star anise in the spice section of your supermarket. Alternatively, you can use 1/8 teaspoon Chinese five-spice powder (also found in the spice section).

Tea-Stained Chicken with Mango Relish

MAKES 4 SERVINGS

In this classic dish, known throughout Asia as Lacquered, or Mahogany, Chicken, a whole chicken is smoked over a blend of spice and tea leaves, then glazed. This method produces a very smoky flavor, which may take some getting used to. Our version uses tea and spice in a gentler fashion, producing a deep "lacquered" look with just a touch of smoky flavor. You can make the tea stain up to one day ahead; store, covered, in an airtight container in the refrigerator.

½ cup water

1 bag black pekoe tea

2 quarter-size slices unpeeled fresh ginger

4 whole black peppercorns

1½ teaspoons tamari or soy sauce

1 teaspoon packed dark brown sugar

2 medium (12-ounce) ripe mangoes, peeled and diced

1 small celery stalk with leaves, minced (about ¼ cup)

1 jalapeño pepper, seeded and minced (wear gloves when handling to prevent irritation)

1 tablespoon minced red onion, rinsed

1 tablespoon fresh lime juice

4 (5-ounce) skinless boneless chicken breast halves

2 teaspoons vegetable oil

1. To prepare the tea stain, bring the water to a boil in a small saucepan. Remove from the heat and add the tea bag, ginger, and peppercorns. Let stand 5 minutes. Squeeze out the tea bag and discard, then add the tamari or soy sauce and brown sugar. Bring the mixture to a boil and continue boiling, stirring frequently, until the liquid is reduced to 2 tablespoons, about 4 minutes. Let cool; remove and discard the ginger and peppercorns.

2. Preheat the oven to 350°F.

3. To prepare the relish, combine the mangoes, celery, jalapeño pepper, onion, and lime juice in a medium bowl.

4. Brush both sides of the chicken with the tea stain. Heat a large nonstick skillet over medium-high heat. Swirl in 1 teaspoon of the oil, then add the chicken. Cook until browned on the bottom, 2 minutes; add the remaining 1 teaspoon oil to the pan and turn the chicken over. When browned on the bottom, about 2 minutes, transfer the skillet to the oven and bake until the chicken is cooked through, 8–9 minutes. Serve with the mango relish.

Per serving (1 breast half with ½ cup relish): 266 Cal, 6 g Fat, 2 g Sat Fat, 77 mg Chol, 208 mg Sod, 21 g Carb, 2 g Fib, 32 g Prot, 33 mg Calc. **POINTS: 5.**

SMART TIP

Rinsing the onion helps take out some of its bite—a great technique whenever you run across an extra-sharp onion or simply want a more mellow onion flavor. Place the onion in a colander and rinse well under cold running water. Pat dry with a paper towel.

Thai Shrimp on Baby Greens

MAKES 4 SERVINGS

If you're short on time and you can't find cooked peeled shrimp at your supermarket's fish counter, look for them in the frozen foods section. Any mixture of greens—such as spinach and endive or mesclun—will work.

⅓ cup fresh lime juice

½ teaspoon salt

1 pound medium-size shrimp, cooked and shelled

2 cucumbers, peeled, quartered lengthwise, seeded, and sliced

½ cup chopped scallions

1 red bell pepper, seeded and cut into thin strips

3 tablespoons dry-roasted peanuts

¼ cup light (reduced-fat) coconut milk

¼ cup nonfat yogurt

¼ teaspoon crushed red pepper

¼ cup chopped fresh cilantro

3 cups baby salad greens

1. Combine the lime juice and salt in a zip-close plastic bag; add the shrimp. Squeeze out the air and seal the bag; turn to coat the shrimp. Refrigerate 30 minutes.

2. Place the cucumber slices in a sieve; let drain 15 minutes.

3. Combine the shrimp, drained cucumbers, scallions, bell pepper, and peanuts in one bowl.

4. Combine the coconut milk, yogurt, and crushed red pepper in another bowl. Drizzle the mixture over the shrimp and vegetables, add the cilantro, and toss gently. Serve the shrimp salad over the baby greens.

Per serving (2 cups): 216 Cal, 6 g Fat, 2 g Sat Fat, 221 mg Chol, 571 mg Sod, 12 g Carb, 3 g Fib, 28 g Prot 136 mg Calc. **POINTS: 4.**

SMART TIP

With the leftover coconut milk, you can make a piña colada smoothie: Combine ¼ cup of light (reduced-fat) coconut milk with 1 cup fresh pineapple chunks and 4 to 6 ice cubes. Pulse until smooth. This filling treat will cost you 2 **POINTS**.

Asian-Style Sea Bass

MAKES 4 SERVINGS

⌐👝 Sea bass—with its silvery blue-green skin, few bones, and lean white flesh—is a much sought-after fish. It's delicately flavored and tasty, and is delicious served hot or cold. Our version infuses bass with the flavors of soy and ginger, to re-create a Chinese-restaurant classic. Substitute grouper, snapper, cod, or even sea scallops if you like.

1 pound sea bass fillets, cut into 4 pieces
3 scallions, thinly sliced
2 tablespoons reduced-sodium soy sauce
1 tablespoon minced peeled fresh ginger
2 teaspoons Asian sesame oil
2 cups cooked white rice

1. Cut out a 12 x 18-inch rectangle of foil. Add the sea bass; top with the scallions, 1 tablespoon of the soy sauce, the ginger, and oil. Fold the foil into a packet, making a tight seal.
2. Bring 1 inch of water to a boil in a large skillet. Add the packet to the water; reduce the heat, cover tightly, and cook about 10 minutes. Open the packet and check the fish; it should be just opaque in the center. If the fish is not fully cooked, reseal the packet and return it to skillet until cooked through. Serve, drizzled with the remaining 1 tablespoon soy sauce, any juices, and the rice.

Per serving (1 fillet with ½ cup rice): 144 Cal, 5 g Fat, 1 g Sat Fat, 47 mg Chol, 384 mg Sod, 2 g Carb, 1 g Fib, 22 g Prot, 34 mg Calc.
POINTS: 3.

SMART TIP

Make a quick veggie dish while the fish cooks by simply placing the fish packet in a large steamer pot (filled with 1 inch of boiling water) instead of a skillet. Then, during the last 5 minutes of cooking time, fill the steamer basket with 1 pound of trimmed asparagus or 2 cups of broccoli florets.

THE DONE DEAL

A fish that "flakes easily with a fork," as many recipes suggest as a test for doneness, is certainly cooked through, but it may be more cooked than you want it to be. The real test for doneness is simple: Fish and shellfish, translucent when raw, are opaque when cooked. To double-check doneness when you're cooking a fillet or steak, pierce it with a fork in its thickest part. The flesh should be just opaque throughout. For whole fish, check that the flesh around the bone looks opaque and pulls away easily. As a general rule, fish fillets or steaks will cook at a rate of 10 minutes per inch when steamed, fried, poached, baked, or grilled. Add a few minutes for each inch of thickness when cooking whole fish. Always check for doneness of whatever kind of fish you're preparing before serving it, and return it to the heat if it's not cooked to your satisfaction.

LIGHTNING QUICK

Faster, fresher, and fewer ingredients—
the buzzwords for the way we
want to cook today. Here are the best
recipes that'll keep you lean, and
the shopping list short, and that are ready
to eat in 30 minutes or less!

Pork with Pineapple and Peppers

MAKES 4 SERVINGS

To save time, ask your butcher to trim and slice the pork, and buy chopped peppers from your supermarket salad bar. Even without these shortcuts, the whole meal still takes fewer than 25 minutes to prepare, start to finish!

¾ pound pork tenderloin, trimmed of all visible fat and sliced into ¼-inch strips

2 teaspoons curry powder

1 teaspoon ground coriander

2 teaspoons canola oil

2 garlic cloves, minced

2 teaspoons minced peeled fresh ginger

1 green bell pepper, seeded and chopped

1 red bell pepper, seeded and chopped

1 (8-ounce) can unsweetened pineapple chunks in juice

2 tablespoons honey

½ teaspoon salt

1 tablespoon chopped fresh cilantro

1. Combine the pork, curry powder, and coriander in a large bowl; set aside.

2. Heat a large nonstick skillet over medium-high heat. Swirl in 1 teaspoon of the oil, then add the garlic and ginger. Cook 30 seconds, and then add the green and red peppers and continue cooking, stirring occasionally, until softened, 4–5 minutes. Transfer to a plate and keep warm.

3. Return the skillet to the heat and add the remaining 1 teaspoon oil. Add the pork mixture and cook, stirring occasionally, until beginning to brown, 3–4 minutes. Add the pineapple chunks and their juice, and the honey. Cook 2 minutes, stirring occasionally. Stir in the peppers and salt, and cook until hot, 2 minutes. Remove from the heat and stir in the cilantro.

Per serving (1 cup): 218 Cal, 6 g Fat, 1 g Sat Fat, 54 mg Chol, 332 mg Sod, 22 g Carb, 2 g Fib, 20 g Prot, 29 mg Calc. **POINTS: 4.**

SMART TIP

Serve this dish with pita bread, mountain bread, or naan—a griddle-cooked Indian flat bread found in gourmet grocery stores and Indian markets.

Spicy Soy Chicken Scallion Stir-fry

MAKES 4 SERVINGS

For stir-fries, look for the bags of precut vegetables—containing broccoli, snow peas, carrots, and red bell peppers—in your supermarket's produce section, next to the prepackaged bags of salad greens.

½ cup uncooked white rice

2 scallions, chopped

¼ cup reduced-sodium chicken broth

3 tablespoons lite soy sauce

2 tablespoons dry sherry

2 tablespoons hoisin sauce

1 tablespoon cornstarch

2 teaspoons sugar

⅛ teaspoon crushed red pepper

2 teaspoons Asian dark sesame oil

1 tablespoon grated peeled fresh ginger

2 garlic cloves, minced

¾ pound chicken breast tenders, halved crosswise

1 (16-ounce) bag precut vegetables for stir-fry

1. Cook the rice according to package directions; remove from the heat, and stir in the scallions.

2. Combine the broth, soy sauce, sherry, hoisin sauce, cornstarch, sugar, and crushed red pepper in a bowl; set aside.

3. Heat a large nonstick skillet over high heat. Swirl in the oil, then add the ginger and garlic. Stir-fry 30 seconds. Add the chicken, and cook until it begins to brown, 2 minutes. Add the vegetables and stir-fry until softened, 3 minutes. Pour in the broth mixture and bring to a boil, tossing well to coat. Cook until the sauce thickens slightly and the vegetables are tender, about 2 minutes more. Serve over the rice.

Per serving (1½ cups over ½ cup rice): 288 Cal, 5 g Fat, 1 g Sat Fat, 47 mg Chol, 555 mg Sod, 35 g Carb, 4 g Fib, 25 g Prot, 74 mg Calc. **POINTS: 5.**

73

SMART TIP

We suggest discarding the packet of very salty sauce that often comes with bags of precut veggies before using them in recipes.

Southwestern Sloppy Joes

MAKES 4 SERVINGS

🍲 🔥 Everyone loves the all–American Sloppy Joe. Our version lends a spicy sophistication to this humble dish by adding mild salsa. If you prefer a little more heat, use hot salsa instead.

1 tablespoon canola oil

1 onion, chopped

1 garlic clove, minced

1 jalapeño pepper, seeded and chopped (wear gloves when handling to prevent irritation)

1 teaspoon chili powder

½ teaspoon dried oregano

¾ pound lean ground turkey breast

1 (7-ounce) can Mexican-style corn, rinsed and drained

1½ cups mild chunky salsa

1 tablespoon packed dark brown sugar

4 hamburger rolls, split

Heat a large nonstick skillet over medium–high heat. Swirl in the oil, then add the onion, garlic, and jalapeño. Cook, stirring occasionally, until softened, about 4 minutes. Add the chili powder and oregano, and cook 1 minute more. Add the turkey and corn, and cook until the mixture is nearly dry, about 4 minutes. Stir in the salsa and sugar and cook, stirring occasionally, until slightly thickened and the turkey is cooked through, 4–5 minutes longer. Spoon over the opened rolls and serve.

Per serving (¾ cup mixture with 1 roll): 385 Cal, 15 g Fat, 3 g Sat Fat, 57 mg Chol, 642 mg Sod, 41 g Carb, 4 g Fib, 23 g Prot, 136 mg Calc. **POINTS: 8.**

SMART TIP

Mexican-style corn, sometimes labeled Mexicorn, is a mixture of corn kernels and bell peppers often flavored with mild Mexican spices and is usually found next to regular canned corn in the grocery store. If you can't find it, plain canned corn will do.

THE WELL-STOCKED PANTRY

If you keep a few key staples on hand, you'll always be ready for dinner, even if the cupboard seems bare.

Flavored olive oils, such as lemon, and balsamic vinegars make for quick-and-easy dressings.

Lentils and split peas cook relatively quickly; so do couscous, bulgur, tabbouleh, quinoa, and rice. Canned beans (kidney, pinto, and black) add flavor (and fiber!) to salads, soups, and burritos.

Tandoori paste from a jar mixed with plain, low-fat yogurt makes a fast and tasty topping for pork, swordfish, and most meats.

Canned juices are useful to have on hand: Reduce vegetable juice to a syrupy consistency and drizzle over vegetables. Pineapple juice makes a yummy dessert topping for low-fat frozen yogurt and sorbet when reduced to a thick consistency.

Sweet potatoes are a quick and flavorful snack and make a great side dish.

Stock up on canned goods such as tomato sauce, chopped and whole tomatoes, tomato puree, tuna, vegetarian chili, unsweetened canned fruit, and chicken and vegetable broth.

Sautéed Tuna with White Bean Salad

MAKES 4 SERVINGS

The flesh of fresh tuna—often a deep red color—is surrounded by dark fatty skin that is usually trimmed at the fish market, then it's sold in pieces or as steaks.

1 (8-ounce) can cannellini beans, rinsed and drained

2 plum tomatoes, sliced

¼ small red onion, sliced

1 tablespoon red-wine vinegar

1 teaspoon mayonnaise

1 teaspoon capers, drained

1 garlic clove, minced

¼ teaspoon crumbled dried sage

4 (5-ounce) tuna steaks

½ teaspoon freshly ground pepper

2 teaspoons olive oil

1 (10-ounce) bag triple-washed spinach, rinsed and torn

4 cups torn arugula leaves

1. Combine the beans, tomatoes, onion, vinegar, mayonnaise, capers, half of the garlic, and the sage in a bowl.

2. Sprinkle the tuna with the pepper. Heat a large nonstick skillet over medium-high heat. Swirl in the oil, and then add the tuna. Cook the tuna until just pink in center, about 5 minutes on each side. Transfer to a plate.

3. Add the spinach, arugula, and the remaining garlic to the same skillet. Sauté until the spinach begins to wilt, about 1 minute.

4. Serve the greens topped with the bean mixture and the tuna steaks.

Per serving (1 steak with ½ cup bean salad): 341 Cal, 11 g Fat, 2 g Sat Fat, 55 mg Chol, 322 mg Sod, 18 g Carb, 8 g Fib, 43 g Prot, 194 mg Calc. **POINTS: 7.**

SMART TIP

You can prepare the bean salad one day ahead and refrigerate it overnight to help bring out its flavors. Just let it stand at room temperature while you prepare the tuna steaks.

THE SHORT-ORDER COOK

Cut down on the time you spend in the kitchen with these tips for streamlining meal-making.

Be a neat freak. If everything is in its place in the pantry, you won't waste precious time hunting for ingredients.

Think in twos. When you're chopping one onion, chop another, and store the extra, well-wrapped, in the fridge to use within a day or two.

Gear up. Use timesaving gadgets that really earn their counter space: Invest in a micro-wave, a food processor, a slow cooker, a pressure cooker, and an immersion blender.

Flash in the pan. If a recipe calls for browning the ingredients first, and then adding others, use a larger pan and cook them all at the same time.

One pot fits all. When cooking pasta and vegetables, add the vegetables to the pasta water a few minutes before the pasta is done; they'll be ready at the same time with less cleanup.

lightning quick

Cajun Crab Cake Sandwiches

MAKES 2 SERVINGS

Take one bite of this crispy, crunchy sandwich, topped with tangy tartar sauce, and you'll think you're tasting a little bit of culinary heaven. But not to worry—even though it has the sinful flavor and texture of fried fare, this meal is surprisingly low in **POINTS**.

1 cup (8 ounces) cooked fresh or frozen crabmeat
½ cup chopped onion
½ cup chopped celery
6 tablespoons cracker meal
2 tablespoons nonfat mayonnaise
½ teaspoon Cajun seasoning blend
2 (1-ounce) hard rolls
Lettuce leaves (optional)
1 tablespoon tartar sauce

1. Combine the crabmeat, onion, celery, 4 tablespoons of the cracker meal, the mayonnaise, and Cajun seasoning in a medium bowl; shape the mixture into 2 small patties.

2. Place the remaining 2 tablespoons cracker meal onto a plate; add the crab patties, turning to coat evenly.

3. Spray a nonstick skillet with nonstick spray; place over medium heat. Add the crab patties, cook, turning once, until brown on both sides.

4. Split the rolls and layer each with the lettuce leaves (if using) and a crab cake; top with the tartar sauce and remaining roll halves.

Per serving (1 sandwich): 351 Cal, 9 g Fat, 2 g Sat Fat, 117 mg Chol, 653 mg Sod, 39 g Carb, 2 g Fib, 28 g Prot, 178 mg Calc. **POINTS: 7.**

SMART TIP
Substitute shredded imitation crabmeat or drained canned crabmeat for the real crabmeat, if you prefer. For virtually **POINTS**-free mock tartar sauce, combine 1½ teaspoons light mayonnaise with ½ teaspoon chopped pickle or relish. (You'll save about 1 **POINT** if you use it in place of the regular tartar sauce.)

Beef Marsala

Top round steak, though flavorful, can easily get tough if overcooked. So try to cook the meat as quickly as possible, and be sure to add it back into the sauce only long enough to heat it through.

- 4 cups (4 ounces) wide egg noodles
- ¾ pound top round steak, about ¼-inch thick, sliced crosswise into 4 pieces
- ½ teaspoon salt
- ¼ teaspoon freshly ground pepper
- 2 teaspoons olive oil
- 1 onion, sliced
- 1 tablespoon all-purpose flour
- 1 (8-ounce) package presliced mushrooms
- ⅓ cup Marsala wine
- ½ cup reduced-sodium chicken broth
- 2 tablespoons chopped fresh parsley

1. Cook the egg noodles according to package directions; drain, and keep warm. Sprinkle the steak with ¼ teaspoon of the salt and ⅛ teaspoon of the pepper.

2. Heat a large nonstick skillet over medium–high heat. Swirl in 1 teaspoon of the oil, then add the beef. Cook until lightly browned, 2 minutes per side. Transfer to a plate; keep warm.

3. Return the skillet to the heat. Add the remaining 1 teaspoon oil, the onion, and flour. Cook, stirring occasionally, 2 minutes. Add the mushrooms and cook until softened, about 4 minutes. Pour in the Marsala, broth, and the remaining ¼ teaspoon salt and the ⅛ teaspoon pepper; bring to a boil. Cook until the sauce thickens slightly, 2 minutes. Add the beef and cook, turning once, until heated through, about 2 minutes. Remove from the heat and stir in the parsley. Serve over the egg noodles.

Per serving (about 1½ cups): 265 Cal, 6 g Fat, 2 g Sat Fat, 69 mg Chol, 394 mg Sod, 27 g Carb, 2 g Fib, 23 g Prot, 27 mg Calc. **POINTS: 5.**

SMART TIP

Beef Marsala also goes nicely over spaetzle, tiny German egg dumplings. Find them in the freezer section (a 1-pound bag is plenty for four). Or serve the dish with tiny steamed red potatoes.

Cuban Black Beans and Rice

MAKES 4 SERVINGS

🔥 If you have leftovers, simply roll the remaining rice and beans into warmed flour tortillas for tasty burritos then top with some salsa and fat-free sour cream.

½ cup uncooked white rice

1 tablespoon olive oil

1 yellow onion, thinly sliced

1 red bell pepper, seeded and thinly sliced

1 green bell pepper, seeded and thinly sliced

3 garlic cloves, minced

5 plum tomatoes, diced, or 1 (14-ounce) can diced tomatoes in juice, drained

2 tablespoons sherry vinegar

1 teaspoon ground cumin

1 teaspoon ground coriander

1 teaspoon dried oregano

1 teaspoon hot pepper sauce

2 (15½-ounce) cans black beans, drained

¼ teaspoon freshly ground pepper

1. Cook the rice according to package directions.

2. Heat a large saucepan or Dutch oven over medium-high heat. Swirl in the oil, then add the onion, red and green bell peppers, and garlic. Cook, stirring occasionally, until softened, about 5 minutes. Stir in the tomatoes, vinegar, cumin, coriander, oregano, and pepper sauce; cook 2 minutes. Add the beans, reduce the heat to medium, cover and simmer until thickened, about 10 minutes. Season with the pepper and serve with the rice.

Per serving (1 cup beans over ½ cup rice): 372 Cal, 5 g Fat, 1 g Sat Fat, 0 mg Chol, 372 mg Sod, 68 g Carb, 4 g Fib, 16 g Prot, 141 mg Calc. **POINTS: 7.**

SMART TIP

This dish takes on another dimension if you use an aromatic rice, such as jasmine or basmati, instead of plain white. If you choose an imported brand, or one bought in bulk, spread the rice out on a plate and pick out any stones or other particles. Then rinse the rice by placing it in a large bowl and filling with cold water. Stir and let the rice settle to the bottom; pour off the water (and any impurities that float to the surface). Repeat.

Chicken Basquaise

MAKES 4 SERVINGS

The preparation for this recipe (a classic dish from the Basque region of southern France and northern Spain) takes less time than the original. The onions and bell peppers are cooked in olive oil until very tender (this mixture is a base for many dishes using chicken and eggs). Our lighter rendition is great over rice or steamed new potatoes.

1 pound skinless boneless chicken breasts, cut into 1-inch pieces
½ teaspoon paprika
½ teaspoon dried basil
½ teaspoon kosher salt
⅛ teaspoon cayenne
Freshly ground pepper, to taste
2 teaspoons extra-virgin olive oil
1 Spanish onion, chopped
1 medium red bell pepper, seeded and chopped
1 medium green bell pepper, seeded and chopped
2 plum tomatoes, chopped
1 garlic clove, minced

1. Place the chicken pieces in a medium bowl. In a small bowl, combine the paprika, basil, salt, cayenne, and pepper. Sprinkle 1 teaspoon of the seasoning mix evenly over the chicken pieces; toss to coat.

2. Heat a large nonstick skillet over medium heat. Swirl in the oil, then add the chicken. Cook until nicely browned and cooked through, 7–8 minutes. Transfer the chicken to a clean bowl.

3. Add the onion and the red and green bell peppers to the skillet; cook until the peppers are tender. Add the chopped tomatoes, the garlic, and the remaining seasoning mix. Cook, stirring, until the tomatoes are softened, about 2 minutes. Stir in the chicken. Cover, reduce the heat to low, and cook until the chicken is heated through, about 10 minutes.

Per serving (2 cups): 200 Cal, 4 g Fat, 1 g Sat Fat, 66 mg Chol, 227 mg Sod, 13 g Carb, 3 g Fib, 28 g Prot, 39 mg Calc. **POINTS: 4.**

SMART TIP

Toasting or cooking herbs and spices in oil helps to quickly intensify their flavors.

Quick Turkey Quesadillas

MAKES 2 SERVINGS

While quesadillas are ordinarily cut into strips or triangles and served as appetizers, our open-face version—loaded with veggies and chunks of turkey—is more of an entrée. Add a dollop of salsa or guacamole for extra flavor.

2 (6-inch) flour tortillas

2 teaspoons vegetable oil

1 cup seeded and minced green bell pepper

½ cup minced red onion

1 teaspoon ground cumin

1 cup canned, low-sodium whole tomatoes, drained and chopped

½ cup (4 ounces) diced skinless, cooked turkey breast

2 tablespoons chopped fresh cilantro

⅛ teaspoon salt

Freshly ground pepper, to taste

1½ ounces Monterey Jack cheese, shredded

1. Preheat the oven to 350°F. Spray a small baking sheet with nonstick spray.

2. Wrap the tortillas in foil; bake until softened, 8–10 minutes. Remove tortillas from oven; increase oven temperature to 375°F.

3. Meanwhile, heat a large nonstick skillet over medium heat. Swirl in the oil, then add the bell pepper and onion. Cook, stirring occasionally, until the vegetables are softened, 3–4 minutes. Add the cumin; cook, stirring constantly, 1 minute. Add the tomatoes, turkey, cilantro, salt, and pepper; cook, stirring occasionally, 3 minutes longer. Remove the skillet from the heat.

4. Unwrap the tortillas and place on the prepared baking sheet. Top with the turkey mixture; sprinkle with the cheese. Bake until the cheese is melted.

Per serving (1 quesadilla): 345 Cal, 17 g Fat, 5 g Sat Fat, 66 mg Chol, 406 mg Sod, 24 g Carb, 3 g Fib, 26 g Prot, 257 mg Calc. **POINTS: 8.**

SMART TIP

If you know you'll be working late and won't have a lot of time to prepare dinner, plan ahead by keeping a few packets of turkey cutlets, strips (for stir-fry), or cubes (for kebabs) in your freezer. They defrost and cook up in a pinch.

Pizza Quattro Stagioni (Four Seasons)

MAKES 4 SERVINGS

Traditionally, this pizza has four distinct sections, each with its own topping. But when a section counts for a whole serving, it's more fun to combine them and sample a little of each topping, as we've done here.

I prebaked thin pizza crust

I canned chopped tomatoes in juice

I tablespoon chopped fresh basil, or 2 teaspoons dried

I tablespoon chopped fresh flat-leaf parsley, or 2 teaspoons dried

1½ teaspoons chopped fresh oregano, or I teaspoon dried

I small garlic clove, minced

Freshly ground pepper, to taste

I cup shredded, reduced-fat mozzarella cheese

I (10-ounce) box frozen artichoke hearts, thawed and squeezed dry

1½ cups sliced mushrooms

12 large black olives, pitted and sliced

2 ounces sliced prosciutto, chopped

1. Preheat the oven according to package directions for the pizza crust.

2. To prepare the sauce, combine the tomatoes, basil, parsley, oregano, garlic, and pepper in a large nonstick skillet. Cook, stirring frequently, until reduced to ½ cup.

3. Leaving a 1½-inch edge, spread the tomato sauce evenly over the crust. Sprinkle with the cheese.

4. Spread the artichoke hearts, mushrooms, olives, and prosciutto evenly over the cheese and tomato sauce. Spray lightly with olive oil nonstick spray; sprinkle with another grating of the pepper. Bake until the crust is golden, and the cheese is bubbling, about 15 minutes.

Per serving (¼ pizza): 370 Cal, 10 g Fat, 4 g Sat Fat, 22 mg Chol, 868 mg Sod, 52 g Carb, 7 g Fib, 20 g Prot, 287 mg Calc. **POINTS: 7.**

SMART TIP

Make a double batch of the pizza sauce by using a 28-ounce can of tomatoes, and doubling the remaining sauce ingredients; simmer about 15 minutes to thicken. Refrigerate half the sauce for another pizza or serve over pasta, fish, or chicken; it will keep up to four days in the refrigerator (or up to two months in an airtight container in the freezer).

lightning quick

Pad Thai

MAKES 6 SERVINGS

Everyone's favorite Thai dish is amazingly easy to make—in Thailand, it's considered street food. Rice sticks, fettucine-like noodles or the thin rice noodles that we feature, can usually be found in the Asian foods section of your supermarket. In case you can't find them in your market, substitute an equal amount of vermicelli or thin spaghetti and cook according to package directions.

8 ounces rice sticks
¼ cup reduced-sodium chicken broth
3 tablespoons ketchup
3 tablespoons fish sauce
1 tablespoon lite soy sauce
1 tablespoon sugar
3 teaspoons peanut oil
1 large egg, lightly beaten
2 garlic cloves, minced
¾ pound large shrimp, peeled and deveined
2 scallions, chopped into ½-inch pieces
2 cups bean sprouts
3 tablespoons chopped unsalted peanuts
6 lime wedges

1. Bring a large pot of water to a boil. Add the rice sticks, and cook 2 minutes; drain.

2. Combine the broth, ketchup, fish sauce, soy sauce, and sugar in a small bowl.

3. Heat a large nonstick skillet over medium-high heat. Swirl in 1 teaspoon of the oil, then add the egg. Cook, stirring, until firm, 2 minutes. Transfer to a bowl.

4. Return the skillet to the heat and add the remaining 2 teaspoons oil. Add the garlic and cook until fragrant, 30 seconds. Add the shrimp and cook, stirring occasionally, until opaque, about 3 minutes. Stir in the scallions, and cook 1 minute. Add the cooked rice stick, the egg, and the broth mixture; cook, tossing well to mix, until hot, about 2 minutes. Remove from the heat, and stir in the bean sprouts. Transfer to a serving plate and sprinkle with the chopped peanuts. Serve with the lime wedges.

Per serving (1½ cups): 248 Cal, 7 g Fat, 1 g Sat Fat, 116 mg Chol, 663 mg Sod, 31 g Carb, 2 g Fib, 10 g Prot, 57 mg Calc. **POINTS: 5.**

SMART TIP

Fish sauce, a dark, pungent, salty sauce made from fermented fish, is a staple in many Southeast-Asian dishes. The Thai version is called *nam pla*, the Vietnamese version, *nuoc nam*; they can be used interchangeably in most recipes. Both can be found in Asian specialty stores and will last for years in the pantry.

Lemony Chicken Couscous

MAKES 2 SERVINGS

Ginger, mint, and lemon not only taste delicious together, they're wonderfully cooling. Try the combination in this quick summer couscous, and you'll be hooked. For a Southwestern twist, substitute equal amounts of lime rind for the lemon rind and cilantro for the fresh mint.

2 medium zucchini, seeded and chopped
1 cup low-sodium chicken broth
½ cup water
2 tablespoons chopped fresh mint
2 tablespoons grated lemon rind
1 teaspoon grated peeled fresh ginger, or ½ teaspoon ground ginger
4 ounces couscous
½ cup cooked shredded chicken breast

1. Combine the zucchini, broth, water, mint, lemon rind, and ginger in a medium saucepan; bring to a boil.

2. Stir in the couscous; remove the saucepan from the heat. Let stand, covered, 5 minutes.

3. Fluff the couscous with a fork, and gently toss with the shredded chicken.

Per serving: 315 Cal, 2 g Fat, 1 g Sat Fat, 26 mg Chol, 67 mg Sod, 52 g Carb, 5 g Fib, 21 g Prot, 60 mg Calc. **POINTS: 6.**

SMART TIP

To seed the zucchini, just halve it lengthwise and scoop out the seeds with a small spoon. To grate a lemon, use a zester or the fine side of a vegetable grater. Wrap the remaining lemon in plastic wrap and refrigerate for use another time.

CHICKEN ON THE RUN

For those weeks when life in the fast lane prevents you from cooking your own chicken, try spicing up a store-bought, precooked rotisserie bird. However, always remove the fattening skin from the bird before eating. Here, some easy meal suggestions:

■ Build a meal around a whole chicken by placing it on top of a bed of quick-cooking grains, such as instant brown or white rice or couscous. Round out the meal with easy-to-make frozen vegetables, such as peas and carrots, or fresh veggies that cook quickly, such as zucchini.

■ Remove the chicken from the bone and shred the meat. To make a simple wrap, place the chicken on a flavored wrap (such as sun-dried tomato or spinach). Add some arugula leaves, and sliced tomato, and roll up.

Top with a dollop of fat-free plain yogurt mixed with your favorite herb (try oregano or tarragon); roll up.

■ Slice a warmed grilled chicken breast and place it over a mixture of cooked bulgur, steamed corn kernels, chopped red onion, and diced tomato; season with freshly ground pepper.

■ Toss chicken breast chunks with cold cooked pasta, your favorite chopped veggies (carrots, celery, and onion work well), and a drizzle of a low-fat vinaigrette (such as raspberry), for a fuss-free pasta salad.

GREAT GRILLING

Though we may not be grilling 24/7 yet, we're firing up the flame more than ever—with deliciously healthy results.

Smoky Gazpacho

MAKES 4 SERVINGS

Gazpacho from the grill? Yes, and it's wonderful!

1 large red onion, quartered

1 large green bell pepper, seeded and quartered

8 large plum tomatoes, halved

3 garlic cloves, chopped

2 tablespoons fresh lime juice

1 tablespoon balsamic or red-wine vinegar

½ teaspoon salt

½ teaspoon freshly ground pepper

Hot pepper sauce (optional)

½ medium cucumber, peeled and chopped

1. Spray the grill rack with nonstick spray; prepare the grill for medium-hot fire.

2. Grill the onion and bell pepper 5 inches from heat, until slightly charred on all sides, 8–10 minutes. Grill the tomatoes, turning once, 2–3 minutes.

3. Combine the onion, bell pepper, tomatoes, garlic, lime juice, vinegar, salt, and pepper in a blender or food processor; puree. Season to taste with pepper sauce (if using) and transfer the gazpacho to a nonreactive bowl. Cover and refrigerate until the soup is chilled, at least 2 hours, or overnight.

4. When ready to serve, sprinkle with the cucumber.

Per serving (1 cup): 62 Cal, 1 g Fat, 0 g Sat Fat, 0 mg Chol, 291 mg Sod, 14 g Carb, 3 g Fib, 2 g Prot, 32 mg Calc. ***POINTS: 1.***

SMART TIP

Plan ahead to use this recipe. Place the onion, bell pepper, and tomatoes alongside whatever you're grilling and voilà, you've got the base for a sensational, zesty summer soup that can be made in minutes the following day.

Tomatoes Grilled with Basil and Garlic

MAKES 4 SERVINGS

Try the large assortment of heirloom tomatoes available from farmers' markets throughout the warm-weather months.

3 garlic cloves, minced

1 tablespoon shredded fresh basil

Pinch salt

1 tablespoon olive oil

4 medium tomatoes or 8 large plum tomatoes, halved lengthwise

4 metal skewers (if using plum tomatoes)

1. Spray the grill rack with nonstick spray; prepare the grill for medium-hot fire.

2. Combine the garlic, basil, salt, and oil in a small bowl.

3. Spoon the herb mixture onto the cut sides of the tomatoes and let stand at room temperature 1 hour. If using plum tomatoes, thread them on skewers.

4. Grill the tomatoes 5 inches from heat, at edge of grill, turning once, until hot, about 10 minutes for medium tomatoes, and 5 minutes for plum tomatoes. Serve the tomatoes hot, or at room temperature.

Per serving (2 medium or 4 plum tomato halves): 57 Cal, 4 g Fat, 1 g Sat Fat, 0 mg Chol, 43 mg Sod, 6 g Carb, 1 g Fib, 1 g Prot, 14 mg Calc. **POINTS: 1.**

SMART TIP

If you don't have fresh basil on hand, substitute it with 1 teaspoon dried basil, oregano, or thyme.

Grilled Red or Sweet White Onions

MAKES 8 SERVINGS

This is a wonderful condiment served right off the grill or chilled and used later in sandwiches or a salad.

6 large red or white onions, cut into ½-inch-thick slices

Spray the grill rack with nonstick spray; prepare the grill for medium-hot fire. Grill onions 5 inches from heat, turning once, until cooked through, 20–25 minutes.

Per serving (½ cup): 35 Cal, 0 g Fat, 0 g Sat Fat, 0 mg Chol, 9 mg Sod, 8 g Carb, 1 g Fib, 1 g Prot, 24 mg Calc. **POINTS: 1.**

SMART TIP

Try grilling an assortment of onions—red, Spanish, or Vidalia—whenever there's room on the grill; they won't go to waste.

Madeira-Flavored Grilled Portobello Mushrooms

It's always a tasty delight to have a supply of grilled portobellos in the refrigerator for a sandwich or to liven up a salad.

¼ cup Madeira wine

1 tablespoon balsamic vinegar

1 tablespoon extra-virgin olive oil

1 tablespoon light tamari or reduced-sodium soy sauce

1 garlic clove, minced

1 tablespoon chopped fresh oregano, or 1 teaspoon dried

1 tablespoon chopped fresh basil, or 1 teaspoon dried

1 tablespoon chopped fresh parsley, or 1 teaspoon dried

4 portobello mushrooms, stems removed

1. Combine the wine, vinegar, oil, tamari or soy sauce, garlic, oregano, basil, and parsley in a zip-close plastic bag; add the mushrooms. Squeeze out the air and seal the bag; turn to coat the mushrooms. Refrigerate, turning the bag occasionally, at least 6 hours or overnight.

2. Spray the grill rack with nonstick spray; prepare the grill for medium-hot fire.

3. Pour the marinade into a small saucepan and boil, stirring constantly, 3 minutes.

4. Grill the mushrooms, stem-side down, 5 inches from heat, turning occasionally, until golden brown on both sides, about 7 minutes. Pour the cooked marinade over the grilled mushrooms and serve.

Per serving (1 mushroom): 69 Cal, 4 g Fat, 1 g Sat Fat, 0 mg Chol, 154 mg Sod, 5 g Carb, 1 g Fib, 2 g Prot, 11 mg Calc. *POINTS: 2.*

SMART TIP

If you don't have Madeira on hand, substitute with red or white wine. Save the mushroom stems, and toss them into the pot to flavor a homemade broth.

Crispy Barbecued Sweet Potatoes

MAKES 4 SERVINGS

These easy-to-prepare sweet potatoes pack a big flavor punch.

3 tablespoons ketchup
1 tablespoon Worcestershire sauce
1 tablespoon red-wine vinegar
1 teaspoon yellow mustard
½ teaspoon freshly ground pepper
1 pound sweet potatoes, peeled and cut into ¼-inch-thick slices

1. Spray the grill rack with nonstick spray; prepare the grill for medium-hot fire.

2. Combine the ketchup, Worcestershire sauce, vinegar, mustard, and pepper in a small bowl; mix well.

3. Brush the potato slices on both sides with the ketchup mixture. Grill the potatoes 5 inches from heat, turning frequently and brushing with the remaining ketchup mixture, until browned on the outside and tender when pierced with a barbecue fork, about 8 minutes.

Per serving (½ cup): 104 Cal, 0 g Fat, 0 g Sat Fat, 0 mg Chol, 188 mg Sod, 24 g Carb, 3 g Fib, 2 g Prot, 25 mg Calc. **POINTS: 1.**

SMART TIP
You can't go wrong serving these tasty spuds alongside grilled chicken and vinegar-tossed broccoli coleslaw.

GET UP AND GRILL

Whether you've never fired up a grill or you just need to hone your skills after a long hiatus, here is everything you ever wanted to know—and then some—about becoming a grill master.

FUEL UP	FLAVOR FACTOR	PERFECT FOR
Gas	Thanks to push-button convenience, expect even, consistent cooking from a gas grill—but no added flavor.	Those who like to grill year-round (gas grills are easy to fire up in the dead of winter), or grill beginners.
Lump Charcoal (avoid briquettes, which contain coal dust and borax)	Some prefer the flavor of fare grilled over live fire, especially those foods cooked with wood chips; and because the charcoal grills give off hotter heat, they produce tastier results when it comes to searing.	Those not afraid of a little fire; the more seasoned backyard gourmet.
Powered Electrically	Nonexistent—because it's a dry-heat source, an electric grill basically broils your food.	Those who live in cities or apartment complexes that don't allow open-fire grills.

Grilled Potato Salad

MAKES 4 SERVINGS

Grilling adds a wonderful flavor dimension to this favorite summertime salad. We've also made it healthier by including plenty of vegetables. If you're in a rush, use presliced potatoes, available in the produce section of your supermarket.

1½ pounds russet potatoes, peeled and cut into ¼-inch-thick slices

1 red onion, peeled and cut into ¼-inch-thick slices

1 pint grape or cherry tomatoes, halved

3 tablespoons chopped fresh parsley

1 tablespoon olive oil

1 tablespoon cider vinegar

1 tablespoon country-style (coarse-grained) Dijon mustard

¼ teaspoon celery seeds

½ teaspoon salt

Freshly ground pepper, to taste

1. Spray the grill rack with nonstick spray; prepare the grill for a medium-hot fire.

2. Spray the potatoes all over with nonstick spray. Place the potatoes on the grill, cover, and grill until the potatoes are tender and well scored with grilling marks, 6–7 minutes per side. Transfer to a bowl. Spray the onion with nonstick spray and grill, uncovered, until tender and well scored with grilling marks, 4–5 minutes per side. Transfer to a cutting board and coarsely chop. Add the onion and the tomatoes to the potatoes.

3. Combine the parsley, oil, vinegar, mustard, celery seeds, salt, and pepper in a small bowl. Pour over the potato mixture and toss well to coat.

Per serving (generous 1¼ cups): 196 Cal, 4 g Fat, 1 g Sat Fat, 0 mg Chol, 358 mg Sod, 38 g Carb, 4 g Fib, 4 g Prot, 33 mg Calc. **POINTS: 3.**

SMART TIP

To make this dish a day ahead, grill the vegetables and assemble the dressing the night before, but don't toss them together. Then refrigerate overnight. The next day, remove the potato mixture from the refrigerator about one hour before serving. When ready to serve, simply toss the potato mixture with the dressing.

Grilled Corn on the Cob with Orange-Basil Butter

MAKES 4 SERVINGS

Grilling corn is a great way to add flavor to corn salads and side dishes; the kernels sweeten as they roast. While the grill is hot, throw on a few more ears of corn to have on hand for recipes that call for canned or frozen corn. Just slice the corn from the cob with a sharp knife, let it cool completely, and freeze in a zip-close freezer bag for up to two months.

4 ears fresh corn
2 tablespoons light margarine spread or light butter, softened
1 teaspoon grated orange rind
½ teaspoon balsamic vinegar
½ teaspoon sugar
½ teaspoon dried basil
½ teaspoon salt
Freshly ground pepper, to taste

1. Spray the grill with nonstick spray; prepare the grill for a medium-hot fire. Husk the corn and remove any corn silk. Lightly spray the corn with nonstick spray and grill, turning occasionally, until tender, about 6 minutes.

2. Meanwhile, combine the margarine or butter, orange rind, vinegar, sugar, basil, salt, and pepper in a small bowl. Brush the grilled corn with the orange-basil butter and serve immediately.

Per serving (1 ear): 111 Cal, 4 g Fat, 1 g Sat Fat, 0 mg Chol, 373 mg Sod, 20 g Carb, 2 g Fib, 3 g Prot, 6 mg Calc. **POINTS: 2.**

SMART TIP

Try some of these great variations on our butter spread: lemon-thyme, cumin-cayenne, or onion-garlic.

SMART GRILLING TIPS

Think safety. Place the grill on a solid, level surface away from the garbage, fences, and trees. Portable models should always be placed on a heat-proof surface.

Start with a clean grill. Use a wire brush to clean the grill after use and remember to empty the ash catcher. If the ash catcher is full, air may not reach the coals. Always trim the fat away from meats and poultry before grilling. Fat drippings catch fire, which is dangerous, and can cause meat or poultry to char.

Avoid cross-contamination between uncooked and cooked foods by always using clean plates when removing food from the grill. Wash tongs if necessary.

Use starter liquid to light coals, not gasoline or kerosene. Adding starter fluid to quick-lighting briquettes or hot coals will cause a flare-up.

Leave the lid open when starting a gas grill.

Place the food on the grill once the flames have stopped jumping up from the coals. Generally, coals will take about 45 minutes to burn down; some coals are ready in as little as 15 minutes, so follow the guidelines on the coal package.

Never leave a grill unattended, particularly if there are children around.

When finished grilling, douse the coals in water, and stir them until the fire is extinguished.

Store propane cylinders upright, out of the sunlight, and away from children.

Grilled Lamb Chops with Tomato-Mint Chutney

MAKES 4 SERVINGS

Lamb is wonderful when grilled, but these chops and chutney are exceptional!
Serve them with couscous. You can prepare the chutney up to two days ahead and
refrigerate it in an airtight container.

1 tablespoon +
  1 teaspoon olive oil
1 onion, chopped
2 garlic cloves,
  minced
4 small plum
  tomatoes, chopped
1 small yellow bell
  pepper, seeded
  and chopped
¼ teaspoon salt
½ teaspoon freshly
  ground pepper
2 tablespoons
  chopped fresh mint
2 tablespoons fresh
  lime juice
⅛ teaspoon crushed
  red pepper
  (optional)
4 (5-ounce) loin lamb
  chops, trimmed of
  all visible fat

1. For the chutney, heat a nonstick skillet. Swirl in the oil, then add onion and garlic. Cook, stirring frequently, until softened, about 2 minutes. Add the tomatoes, bell pepper, a pinch of salt, and ¼ teaspoon of the pepper. Cook, stirring, until the bell pepper is crisp-tender, about 3 minutes. Remove from heat.

2. Transfer the vegetable mixture to a small bowl. Add the mint, lime juice, and crushed red pepper (if using); stir, and set aside.

3. Spray the grill rack with nonstick spray; prepare the grill for medium-hot fire. Season the lamb with the remaining salt and ¼ teaspoon pepper.

4. Grill the lamb 5 inches from heat, turning once, 4–5 minutes (rare), 6–7 minutes (medium), 8–9 minutes (well-done).

5. Spoon ½ cup of chutney over each chop and serve.

Per serving (1 chop with ½ cup chutney): 245 Cal, 13 g Fat, 4 g Sat Fat, 81 mg Chol, 211 mg Sod, 5 g Carb, 1 g Fib, 26 g Prot, 29 mg Calc.
POINTS: 6.

SMART TIP

Scent the smoke by adding fresh herbs (thyme and rosemary will lend a wonderful aroma to lamb and pork) or cracked nuts (such as walnuts or hazelnuts) to the coals. Soak herbs or nuts in water for 30 minutes prior to grilling; they'll burn more slowly in the coals.

Kansas City–Style BBQ Chicken

MAKES 6 SERVINGS

Sweet barbecue sauce is what gives Kansas City–style barbecue its distinct flavor, and it tastes heavenly on chicken. Try butterflying the chicken first—it takes only minutes and helps the bird grill more evenly. Keep the skin on while you grill the bird to shield it from the heat. Then, when the chicken is nearly cooked, remove the skin and brush on the tangy barbecue sauce for a finger-licking, low-fat finish!

2 teaspoons paprika
1¾ teaspoons garlic powder
2½ teaspoons chili powder
1 teaspoon salt
Freshly ground pepper, to taste
1 (3½ to 4-pound) chicken, trimmed of visible fat but not skinned
1 cup ketchup
5 teaspoons molasses
1 tablespoon packed dark brown sugar
1½ teaspoons Worcestershire sauce
1¼ teaspoons dry mustard

1. Spray the grill rack with nonstick spray; prepare the grill for indirect heating.

2. Combine the paprika, 1¼ teaspoons of the garlic powder, 2 teaspoons of the chili powder, the salt, and pepper in a bowl.

3. Cut out the chicken's backbone with poultry shears. Open the chicken out flat, skin-side up. With your fingers, loosen the skin over the breasts, legs, and thighs, and spread the paprika mixture under the skin. Let stand 15 minutes.

4. Meanwhile, in a small saucepan combine the ketchup, molasses, brown sugar, Worcestershire sauce, mustard, and the remaining ½ teaspoon each garlic powder and chili powder. Bring to a simmer over medium heat; reduce the heat to low and simmer 5 minutes, stirring often.

5. Place the chicken, skin-side up, over the indirect heat section of the grill. Grill 20 minutes, turn, and grill 20 minutes longer. Turn the chicken skin-side up; carefully remove the skin with tongs and discard. Grill the chicken 10 minutes more. Brush the chicken with half of the sauce and continue grilling until an instant-read thermometer registers 165°F when inserted into the thickest part of the breast, and 170°F when inserted into the thickest part of the thigh, 10–15 minutes longer. Remove from the grill, cover loosely with foil, and let stand 5 minutes before cutting into serving pieces. Cut each breast half horizontally in half. Serve with the remaining sauce.

Per serving (one halved breast half, or one leg, with about 3 tablespoons sauce): 226 Cal, 6 g Fat, 2 g Sat Fat, 77 mg Chol, 839 mg Sod, 15 g Carb, 1 g Fib, 27 g Prot, 42 mg Calc. **POINTS: 5.**

SMART TIP

When barbecuing, never add the barbecue sauce until the last few minutes of cooking. The sugars in the sauce tend to burn over long cooking times, ruining the good barbecue flavor you were trying to develop.

Veggie Burgers

MAKES 4 SERVINGS

These meatless patties can be formed a day ahead, then wrapped individually and refrigerated overnight until you're ready to grill them.

1½ cups quartered shiitake or white mushrooms

1 cup uncooked quick-cooking brown rice

1 small onion, chopped

¾ cup canned kidney beans, rinsed and drained

1 carrot, shredded

1 cup shredded reduced-fat mozzarella cheese

¼ cup grated Parmesan cheese

2 egg whites

2 tablespoons tomato paste

½ teaspoon salt

⅛ teaspoon freshly ground pepper

1. Spray the grill rack with nonstick spray; prepare the grill for medium-hot fire.

2. Combine the mushrooms, rice, onion, and beans in a food processor and pulse until finely chopped. Transfer the mixture to a bowl. Add the carrot, mozzarella, Parmesan, egg whites, tomato paste, salt, and pepper; toss to combine. Form the mixture into 4 burgers.

3. Grill the burgers 5 inches from heat, turning once, until cooked through, 4–5 minutes on each side.

Per serving (1 burger): 278 Cal, 8 g Fat, 4 g Sat Fat, 18 mg Chol, 821 mg Sod, 34 g Carb, 6 g Fib, 20 g Prot, 405 mg Calc. **POINTS: 5.**

SMART TIP

The crinkle cutter is a nifty gadget that can help you create an impressive array of "fries" cut from your favorite vegetables, including potatoes, carrots, zucchini, and sweet potatoes. It's available at most houseware stores.

GRILLING ESSENTIALS

Charcoal Chimney Starter: A cylindrical metal container gets the charcoal going more easily. Place the briquettes in the top, add crumpled newspaper to the bottom, and light. The coals take 25 minutes to be ready for grilling. Simply turn out the hot coals into the grill.

Gas Igniter: This is a long-barreled gas match that safely lights charcoal.

Long-Handled Tongs: A must-have for turning food on the grill, moving coals, and for preventing burns.

Long-Handled Fork: Indispensable for turning chicken.

Fireproof Gloves: Use these gloves when picking up metal skewers that have been on the grill.

Wire Brush: This is the easiest way to keep the grill clean. The brush's wire bristles can be used to scrape off any residue left on the grill after cooking. It can also be used to clean off the grill while it is still hot, which is excellent when grilling more than one food.

Southwest Grilled Chicken with Pineapple Salsa

MAKES 4 SERVINGS

Pineapple and crisp jicama lend a juicy crunch to this unusual salsa—a good match for a simple cumin-rubbed grilled chicken. If you like your salsa a little more fiery, leave the seeds in the jalapeño. The salsa can be made up to one day ahead; just cover and refrigerate.

2 teaspoons ground cumin
¾ teaspoon salt
1¼ teaspoons sugar
4 (5-ounce) skinless boneless chicken breast halves
1 teaspoon olive or vegetable oil
2 cups (about 12 ounces) canned diced pineapple
2 cups (about 12 ounces) diced jicama
¼ orange bell pepper or red bell pepper, seeded and finely chopped
½ jalapeño pepper, seeded and minced (wear gloves when handling to prevent irritation)
3 tablespoons rice vinegar
2 tablespoons finely chopped sweet onion
1 tablespoon rum (optional)

1. Spray the grill rack or a ridged grill pan with nonstick spray; prepare the grill or set the grill pan over medium-high heat.
2. Combine the cumin, ½ teaspoon of the salt, and ¼ teaspoon of the sugar in a small bowl. Brush the chicken all over with the oil; sprinkle with the spice mixture.
3. Grill the chicken until browned and cooked through, turning once halfway through, 10–12 minutes.
4. Meanwhile, toss together the pineapple, jicama, bell pepper, jalapeño pepper, vinegar, onion, rum (if using), and the remaining 1 teaspoon sugar and ¼ teaspoon salt in a medium bowl. Serve with the chicken.

Per serving (1 breast half with 1 scant cup salsa): 266 Cal, 6 g Fat, 1 g Sat Fat, 77 mg Chol, 514 mg Sod, 22 g Carb, 6 g Fib, 32 g Prot, 46 mg Calc. **POINTS: 5.**

SMART TIP

Jicama (HEE-kuh-muh)—a large, tan turnip-shaped tuber—has crisp, juicy flesh similar to a water chestnut. Used in many Mexican dishes, it adds a welcome crunch to salsas, salads, and stir-fries—and it makes a great addition to a crudités platter. When buying jicama, choose one that is firm to the touch with an unbruised tan peel. To dice, peel and slice the jicama into ¼-inch-thick rounds, stack the rounds on top of one another, and slice into ¼-inch strips. Then cut across the strips to dice.

Lime-Glazed Grilled Chicken with Tomato-Avocado Salad

MAKES 4 SERVINGS

The salad element of this dish can be made two different ways. If you'd like the avocado to retain its shape, choose one that is just ripe but not too soft to the touch. Cut and add it to the salad immediately before serving. If you prefer, use a soft, well-ripened avocado, and add it at any time. The buttery-soft avocado pieces will partially "melt" into the tomato and the lime juices, creating an avocado vinaigrette. Be sure to choose smooth-skinned Florida avocados, as they have significantly less fat in their flesh than the dark, pebbly-skinned Haas avocados grown in California.

2 cups halved red cherry tomatoes

1 cup halved yellow cherry tomatoes

3 scallions, chopped

3 tablespoons chopped fresh cilantro

5 tablespoons fresh lime juice

½ jalapeño pepper, seeded and minced (wear gloves when handling to prevent irritation)

1 teaspoon salt

Pinch sugar

1 small (10-ounce) Florida avocado, pitted, peeled, and cut into ½-inch dice

4 (5-ounce) skinless boneless chicken breast halves

1 teaspoon olive or vegetable oil

Freshly ground pepper, to taste

2 tablespoons apple jelly

1. Spray the grill rack or a ridged grill pan with nonstick spray; prepare the grill or set the grill pan over medium-high heat.

2. Toss the red and yellow tomatoes, scallions, cilantro, 3 tablespoons of the lime juice, the jalapeño pepper, ½ teaspoon of the salt, and the sugar in a large bowl. Add the avocado and gently toss to combine.

3. Brush the chicken all over with the oil; sprinkle with the remaining ½ teaspoon salt and the pepper.

4. To prepare the lime glaze, microwave the jelly with the remaining 2 tablespoons lime juice in a microwavable glass cup measure on High until it just reaches a boil, 30–40 seconds.

5. Grill the chicken 4 minutes per side. Then brush the chicken with the glaze and continue grilling, brushing frequently, until browned and cooked through, 2–4 minutes more. Serve with the salad.

Per serving (1 breast half with ¾ cup salad): 360 Cal, 17 g Fat, 3 g Sat Fat, 77 mg Chol, 682 mg Sod, 21 g Carb, 7 g Fib, 34 g Prot, 47 mg Calc. **POINTS: 8**.

SMART TIP

The glaze should be brushed on only when the chicken is nearly cooked; the sugars in the glaze will burn if exposed to the high heat of the grill for too long. For really moist chicken, remove it from the grill at the shorter cooking time and immediately wrap all four breasts together in a large piece of foil; let stand 5 minutes. Unwrap and serve.

North Carolina BBQ Pork Tenderloin with Mop Sauce

MAKES 6 SERVINGS

North Carolinians marinate their barbecued meats with a dry spice rub, then serve them bathed in a vinegary, spicy sauce that gets "mopped up" with a piece of bread. Though pork is the meat of choice in this recipe, the tasty spice rub also works well on chicken, beef, or even catfish.

2 tablespoons packed dark brown sugar
1 tablespoon paprika
1 tablespoon chili powder
1½ teaspoons ground cumin
1 teaspoon salt
¼ teaspoon cayenne
Freshly ground pepper, to taste
⅓ cup ketchup
¼ cup cider vinegar
2 tablespoons molasses
2 teaspoons Worcestershire sauce
2 pork tenderloins (1½ pounds), trimmed of all visible fat

1. Spray the grill rack with nonstick spray; prepare the grill for indirect heating.

2. To prepare the spice rub, combine the brown sugar, paprika, chili powder, cumin, salt, cayenne, and pepper in a bowl. Rub half of the mixture all over the pork and let stand 15 minutes.

3. Meanwhile, to prepare the Mop Sauce, combine the ketchup, vinegar, molasses, and Worcestershire sauce in a bowl.

4. Rub the pork with the remaining spice rub. Place over the indirect heat section of the grill. Grill 15 minutes. Turn the pork and grill until an instant-read thermometer inserted into the center of the meat registers 160°F, 12–15 minutes longer. Remove from the grill, cover loosely with foil, and let stand 10 minutes before slicing. Serve with the Mop Sauce.

Per serving (3 ounces meat with about 2 tablespoons sauce): 210 Cal, 5 g Fat, 2 g Sat Fat, 72 mg Chol, 630 mg Sod, 15 g Carb, 1 g Fib, 26 g Prot, 40 mg Calc. *POINTS: 4.*

SMART TIP

Leftovers from this recipe will make great pulled-pork sandwiches. Just thinly slice or chop the pork and combine with the leftover sauce in a small saucepan. Cook over low heat, stirring often, just until the meat is hot, and serve on soft sandwich rolls with sweet gherkin pickles on the side.

great grilling

Lime-Grilled Swordfish

Select swordfish steaks of even thickness for perfectly grilled fish. And if you don't have vermouth on hand, use white wine or even tequila!

¼ cup dry vermouth

2 tablespoons fresh lime juice

1 tablespoon minced fresh cilantro

1 tablespoon extra-virgin olive oil

1 tablespoon light tamari or reduced-sodium soy sauce

½ teaspoon freshly ground pepper

4 (5-ounce) swordfish steaks, about 1-inch thick

1. Spray the grill rack with nonstick spray; prepare the grill for medium-hot fire.

2. Combine the vermouth, lime juice, cilantro, oil, tamari or soy sauce, and pepper in a zip-close plastic bag; add the swordfish steaks. Squeeze out the air and seal the bag; turn to coat the steaks. Refrigerate, turning the bag occasionally, at least 1 hour.

3. Grill the swordfish 5 inches from heat, turning once, until the fish is just opaque in the center, about 8 minutes.

4. Meanwhile, pour the marinade into a small saucepan and boil, stirring constantly, 3 minutes. Spoon the cooked marinade over the grilled fish and serve.

Per serving (1 steak): 225 Cal, 9 g Fat, 2 g Sat Fat, 55 mg Chol, 349 mg Sod, 2 g Carb, 0 g Fib, 29 g Prot, 9 mg Calc. **POINTS: 5.**

SMART TIP

Make a leek or herb brush for coating food on the grill with marinade. For a leek brush, cut 2-inch vertical slices into the green end of a leek and spread out the leek top to form a brush. For an herb brush, tie a string around the ends of four to six sprigs of rosemary and thyme, and spread out the sprigs to make a brush.

THAT'S ENTERTAINMENT

Here's foolproof company
and holiday fare that's easy on
the cook and delicious.

Crab, Pear, and Cheese Strudel

MAKES 4 SERVINGS

With a light, crispy phyllo crust, this strudel has a delectably rich filling of savory and sweet ingredients. Creamy melted mozzarella cheese and crispy water chestnuts add scrumptious texture and crunch.

2 small pears, cored, peeled, and chopped

½ pound jumbo lump crabmeat, picked over

¾ cup coarsely grated skim-milk mozzarella cheese

½ cup finely chopped lean Virginia ham

¾ cup minced drained water chestnuts

6 scallions, thinly sliced

1 tablespoon fresh lemon juice

¼ teaspoon crushed red pepper

6 (12 x 17-inch) sheets phyllo, thawed according to package directions

4 teaspoons vegetable oil

1 teaspoon plain dried bread crumbs

Come to Brunch
MENU

Crab, Pear, and Cheese Strudel

Peppery Popovers

Warm Salad of Wild Mushrooms and Fennel

Tenderloin of Beef with Blue Cheese and Herb Crust

Rösti Potatoes with Celeriac

Carrot Cake

1. Preheat the oven to 375°F. Spray a 10 x 15-inch jelly-roll pan with nonstick spray.
2. For filling, combine the pears, crabmeat, cheese, ham, water chestnuts, scallions, lemon juice, and crushed red pepper in a bowl.
3. Place 1 phyllo sheet onto a 16-inch sheet of wax paper and brush evenly with ½ teaspoon of the oil. Top with the remaining sheets of phyllo, brushing each sheet with ½ teaspoon oil. Sprinkle the top phyllo sheet evenly with the bread crumbs.
4. Spoon the filling, lengthwise, about 1 inch from a long side of the phyllo stack. Fold the 1 inch of dough over the filling, and then fold in 1 inch of the short edges. Roll up the strudel, using the wax paper to help lift the dough. Transfer the roll to the pan; brush with the remaining 1 teaspoon oil. With a sharp knife, lightly cut the top to indicate 4 portions, being careful not to cut all the way through. Bake the strudel until lightly browned and heated through, 15–20 minutes. Let cool 10 minutes, and then cut at the marks and serve.

Per serving (¼ of the strudel): 306 Cal, 9 g Fat, 2 g Sat Fat, 66 mg Chol, 604 mg Sod, 32 g Carb, 4 g Fib, 23 g Prot, 162 mg Calc. **POINTS: 6.**

SMART TIP

You can usually find phyllo in the freezer section of your super-market, but it must be fully thawed before using. Store unopened phyllo in the refrigerator for up to one month. Once the package has been opened, try to use the phyllo within a few days.

Peppery Popovers

MAKES 8 SERVINGS

Popovers puff and rise spectacularly in the oven as the moisture in the batter heats and turns into steam. Take care not to open the oven door and let the steam escape while popovers are baking! If you're a real pepper fan, add about ½ teaspoon to the batter.

2 large eggs
1 cup fat-free milk
1 cup all-purpose flour
½ teaspoon salt
Freshly ground pepper, to taste

1. Preheat the oven to 450°F. Spray an 8-cup popover pan or muffin tin with nonstick spray.

2. With an electric mixer at medium speed, beat the eggs until frothy. Beat in the milk, flour, salt, and pepper.

3. Spoon ¼ cup batter into each cup. Bake 15 minutes; reduce the oven temperature to 400°F and bake until browned, about 12 minutes longer. Serve immediately.

Per serving (1 popover): 86 Cal, 1 g Fat, 0 g Sat Fat, 54 mg Chol, 177 mg Sod, 14 g Carb, 0 g Fib, 4 g Prot, 46 mg Calc. **POINTS: 2.**

SMART TIP

Because no fancy ingredients are needed, consider these popovers a great last-minute addition to round out your favorite soup or stew supper.

BRUNCH: DIETER'S DELIGHT OR DILEMMA?

After first gaining popularity nearly 20 years ago, brunch still remains a tasty tradition today. No big surprise there—who doesn't love simple comfort foods and good company? But brunch can be a tough call when you're playing the weight game. Not only are you often faced with a table full of high-fat temptations (gooey pastries and cheesy quiches come to mind), you've also skipped breakfast, so you're bound to overindulge. Here, several rules for healthy brunching:

Smart Start: If you know that skipping meals triggers overeating for you, eat a small breakfast to hold you over until the main event. Cereal and fat-free milk or fruit are your best bets.

Beware of the Buffet: *All you can eat* are four words that just don't jibe with any healthy-eating plan. Instead, select one item from each food group and center your meal around fresh fruits and vegetables. Treat yourself to one small sweet roll or pastry if you don't go out to brunch often—eat it slowly and savor the sweetness.

Make It a Spritzer: Mimosas and Bloody Marys often flow freely at brunch. But traversing the brunch spread while tipsy is a surefire way to loose your inhibitions and eat more than you should. Limit yourself to one cocktail or opt for sparkling water with a twist instead.

Slow Down: Eat slowly and enjoy your meal. And, most important, pay attention to when you're hungry and when you're full.

Warm Salad of Wild Mushrooms and Fennel

A wonderful assortment of wild mushrooms are now available in most supermarkets. Look for cremini, oyster, chanterelle, and shiitake mushrooms—they all work well in this recipe—but buy whatever is fresh.

1 small fennel bulb, thinly sliced

⅔ cup torn radicchio, rinsed

1 head garlic, cloves separated and peeled

1½ tablespoons extra-virgin olive oil

2½ cups wild mushrooms, sliced and quartered

1¼ cups low-sodium chicken broth

½ cup chopped sun-dried tomatoes (not oil-packed)

6 kalamata olives, pitted and sliced

2 tablespoons minced fresh sage

1½ tablespoons capers, drained

3 tablespoons fresh lemon juice

⅓ medium red bell pepper, seeded and sliced

Freshly ground pepper, to taste

1. Combine the fennel in a small saucepan with enough water to cover and bring to a boil. Reduce the heat, cover, and simmer until the fennel is barely tender, about 5 minutes. Drain, cool, and gently toss with the radicchio in a bowl.

2. Combine the garlic cloves with enough water to cover them by 1 inch in the saucepan, and bring to a boil. Drain the garlic, and repeat the process using fresh water. Reserve the garlic.

3. Heat a nonstick skillet over medium-high heat. Swirl in the oil, then add the garlic. Cook until golden brown, 4–5 minutes. Add the mushrooms and cook until tender, about 8 minutes. Add the broth; cook, scraping up the browned bits from the bottom of the pan, until the broth has almost completely evaporated, 5–10 minutes. Remove from the heat and stir in the tomatoes, olives, sage, and capers.

4. Arrange the fennel and radicchio on plates and top with the mushroom mixture. Drizzle the salad with the lemon juice. Sprinkle with the bell pepper and pepper; serve immediately.

Per serving (1 cup): 160 Cal, 8 g Fat, 1 g Sat Fat, 2 mg Chol, 400 mg Sod, 20 g Carb, 4 g Fib, 7 g Prot, 96 mg Calc. **POINTS: 3.**

SMART TIP

In this recipe, whole garlic cloves are blanched twice before being browned in oil. This technique mellows and softens the garlic cloves enough to be eaten whole. To peel the garlic cloves, lightly crush them with the side of a large knife. The peels should slip off easily.

Rösti Potatoes with Celeriac

MAKES 4 SERVINGS

Swiss rösti (pronounced ROOSH-tee) are crispy golden potato pancakes. In this variation, celeriac gives the rösti an unusual twist. Rösti may be prepared as individual cakes, as in this recipe, but it is also traditional to prepare large cakes and slice them into wedges. Rösti are especially complementary to roast pork.

1 medium (½-pound) russet potato, peeled
1 small (½-pound) celeriac, peeled
1½ teaspoons Dijon mustard
¼ teaspoon crushed black peppercorns
2 teaspoons olive oil

1. Preheat the oven to 475°F. Grate the potato and celeriac and combine with the mustard and peppercorns in a bowl. Divide the mixture into 8 even mounds.

2. Heat a nonstick skillet over medium-high heat. Swirl in 1 teaspoon of the oil, then transfer 4 of the mounds to the skillet and press with a spatula to form 4 patties, about ½-inch thick. Cook the rösti until golden brown, about 1½ minutes per side. Repeat with the remaining oil and potato mixture.

3. Transfer the rösti to a nonstick baking sheet. Bake until heated through, about 5 minutes. Serve immediately.

Per serving (2 patties): 100 Cal, 3 g Fat, 0 g Sat Fat, 0 mg Chol, 36 mg Sod, 11 g Carb, 2 g Fib, 2 g Prot, 18 mg Calc. **POINTS: 2.**

SMART TIP

Celeriac, also known as celery root or celery knob, tastes like a cross between celery and parsley. It combines particularly well with potatoes. Choose firm celeriac with a minimum of knobs. Peel it with a paring knife, cutting away the knobs and tough skin to reach the tender white flesh beneath.

weight watchers

Tenderloin of Beef with Blue Cheese and Herb Crust

MAKES 4 SERVINGS

A savory blue cheese and herb bread crumb topping is a delicious accent to beef tenderloin medallions. The beauty of this impressive dish is that it is incredibly simple to make.

2 slices white bread, crusts removed, toasted

3 tablespoons crumbled blue cheese

2 tablespoons chopped fresh parsley

2 tablespoons chopped fresh chives

Freshly ground black pepper, to taste

½ cup prepared demi-glace sauce

2 tablespoons Madeira wine

1 teaspoon vegetable oil

4 (3-ounce) center-cut beef tenderloin medallions

1. Preheat the oven to 400°F. Crumble the toast into a bowl and blend to a coarse paste with the blue cheese, parsley, chives, and pepper.

2. To prepare the Madeira sauce, combine the demi-glace and wine in a small saucepan. Bring the sauce to a boil, reduce the heat to low, and keep hot.

3. Spray the rack of a roasting pan with nonstick spray. Heat a large nonstick skillet over high heat. Swirl in the oil, then wipe the pan with a paper towel to absorb the excess. Sear the medallions until just browned, about 1 minute per side.

4. Arrange the medallions on the roasting rack. Coat the top side of each medallion with the blue cheese mixture. Roast until the crust is golden brown and the meat is done to taste, 3–4 minutes for medium-rare. Serve the medallions on a pool of warm Madeira sauce.

Per serving (1 medallion with ¼ of the sauce): 254 Cal, 13 g Fat, 5 g Sat Fat, 77 mg Chol, 291 mg Sod, 7 g Carb, 0 g Fib, 26 g Prot, 60 mg Calc. **POINTS: 6.**

SMART TIP

Demi-glace is an intensely flavored, classic French brown veal sauce. It takes many hours to make demi-glace from scratch, but today's home cooks are fortunate in that well-stocked supermarkets and gourmet groceries now carry prepared demi-glace. It can be purchased frozen or as a shelf-stable concentrate. Follow package directions to reconstitute concentrated demi-glace. You can find demi-glace in gourmet stores and better supermarkets.

Carrot Cake

For a pretty presentation that's ready in a flash, cover the baked cake with a paper doily and then dust it with confectioners' sugar. After dusting, carefully lift away the doily, leaving the sugared design intact.

¾ cup all-purpose flour

⅔ cup whole-wheat flour

1 teaspoon baking soda

1 teaspoon baking powder

1 teaspoon cinnamon

1 cup + 2 tablespoons granulated sugar

½ cup vegetable oil

2 large eggs

4 medium carrots, peeled and grated (2 cups)

1 cup drained canned crushed pineapple or pineapple tidbits (no sugar added)

½ cup raisins

2 egg whites

¼ cup confectioners' sugar

1. Preheat the oven to 350°F. Line a 9-inch square cake pan with parchment or wax paper; lightly spray with nonstick spray, and dust with flour.

2. Sift together the all-purpose flour, whole-wheat flour, baking soda, baking powder, and cinnamon in a bowl.

3. Beat the granulated sugar, oil, and eggs until smooth in a bowl. Add the flour mixture and stir until just combined. Stir in the carrots, pineapple, and raisins.

4. With an electric mixer on medium speed, beat the egg whites in a large bowl until they form medium peaks, 3–5 minutes. Using a whisk, gently stir ⅓ of the whites into the batter to lighten it. With a rubber spatula, gently fold in the remaining whites. Pour the batter into the pan and bake until a toothpick inserted in the center of the cake comes out clean, about 45 minutes.

5. Cool in the pan on a rack 10 minutes; remove the cake from the pan and finish cooling on the rack. Dust with confectioners' sugar.

Per serving (1/16 of cake): 198 Cal, 8 g Fat, 1 g Sat Fat, 27 mg Chol, 124 mg Sod, 31 g Carb, 2 g Fib, 3 g Prot, 20 mg Calc. **POINTS: 4.**

SMART TIP

To make ahead, prepare cake as directed except do not dust with confectioners' sugar. Wrap well and freeze up to two weeks. Thaw at room temperature.

Crown Roast of Lamb with Spinach-Orzo Stuffing

MAKES 8 SERVINGS

Don't let this dish's regal name deceive you. It's easy to make—your butcher can actually do most of the work. Ask for the racks to be trimmed of as much external fat as possible, and have the shards of tissue from the lower ends of the bones scraped off, or "Frenched," so they won't burn in the oven. Tying the rack together is also fairly simple, but the butcher can do that, too, if you prefer. Feel free to pick up the chops with your fingers—there's just something about nibbling on them that brings out the medieval king in all of us.

2 lamb rib roast racks, 8 ribs each, well-trimmed (about 2¾ pounds total)
½ lemon
1 teaspoon salt
Freshly ground pepper, to taste
½ medium onion, finely chopped
2 garlic cloves, minced
1 (10-ounce) package frozen chopped spinach, thawed and squeezed dry
2 cups orzo, cooked
½ cup chopped fresh parsley
1 large egg, lightly beaten
2 ounces feta cheese, crumbled (about ¼ cup)
Grated rind of 1 lemon
1 tablespoon dried oregano
16 decorative paper frills (optional)
1 pint cherry or grape tomatoes

> **Spring Dinner**
> **MENU**
>
> Crown Roast of Lamb with Spinach-Orzo Stuffing
>
> Steamed Baby Carrots and Sugar Snap Peas*
>
> Steamed New Potatoes*
>
> Anise-Sesame Cookies
>
> *No recipe

1. Place the oven rack in the lower third of the oven. Preheat the oven to 375°F. Spray a 1-quart baking dish with nonstick spray.

2. Slice the lamb between each rib, cutting almost but not completely through to the bottom. Form the racks into half circles and place together to form a circle, bone-side to center. (If your circle looks more like an oval, turn the rack over and press down with your thumbs to round it out a little more.) Tie the ends together with kitchen string to make a "crown." Rub the lamb with the lemon half, then sprinkle with ½ teaspoon of the salt and a grinding of the pepper. Place in a medium roasting pan and roast 20 minutes.

3. Meanwhile, spray a medium nonstick skillet with nonstick spray and set over medium heat. Add the onion and cook until softened, about 4 minutes. Add the garlic and cook until fragrant, about 30 seconds. Let cool.

4. Combine the spinach, orzo, parsley, egg, feta, lemon rind, oregano, the remaining ½ teaspoon of the salt, and a few grindings of the pepper in a large bowl; add the onion-garlic mixture and stir lightly to blend.

5. Remove the lamb from the oven and stuff the cavity with about 2 cups of the stuffing. Spread the rest of the stuffing in the prepared baking dish, and cover with foil. Bake until an instant-read thermometer inserted into a thick lamb chop, and in both stuffings, registers 145°F, about 20 minutes

continued

more. Remove from the oven, cover loosely with foil, and let stand 10 minutes. Place the lamb on a serving platter and decorate each chop with a paper frill (if using). Serve with the remaining stuffing from the baking pan. Garnish with the tomatoes.

Per serving (2 lamb chops with ½ cup stuffing): 234 Cal, 10 g Fat, 4 g Sat Fat, 84 mg Chol, 502 mg Sod, 15 g Carb, 2 g Fib, 20 g Prot, 103 mg Calc. **POINTS: 5.**

SMART TIP

This yummy stuffing also goes well with poultry. It makes enough to stuff a 4-pound chicken or a small turkey (12 pounds or less). You can also make it as a side dish for other meals. Spray a 1½-quart baking dish with nonstick spray, fill it with stuffing, cover with foil, and bake until hot, 30–45 minutes.

FINISHING TOUCHES

■ Something as spectacular as a crown roast deserves a beautiful vegetable accompaniment. Seek out the freshest baby carrots you can find (try your local farmers' market); then peel and steam them until crisp and tender, about 12 minutes. They need nothing more than a generous sprinkle of fresh, chopped mint.

■ Sugar snap peas are another sweet taste of spring. Just snap off the tips, pulling out any strings if necessary, and steam only until they turn bright green, sometimes less than a minute. Toss them with a drizzle of walnut oil or a light sprinkling of slivered almonds. For a nice combination of sweet and sour, toss the cooked beans with some pickled baby onions, or with equal parts honey and Dijon mustard.

■ Steamed red potatoes complete the meal; select the tiniest ones, with skins that rub off easily. Steam them over two inches of boiling water until they can just be pierced with a skewer (don't overcook—they'll continue cooking off the heat). Immediately toss them with some chopped fresh dill and a little melted butter or olive oil.

Anise-Sesame Cookies

These easy-to-make crisp wafers are made with fragrant sesame and anise seeds, a touch of cinnamon, and heart-healthy olive oil instead of butter. Make them a day or two ahead—their flavor becomes even more complex with time.

⅓ cup olive oil

1 teaspoon anise seeds

1 teaspoon sesame seeds

½ cup sugar

½ teaspoon grated lemon rind

½ teaspoon grated orange rind

2 tablespoons fresh lemon juice

2 tablespoons fresh orange juice

1 teaspoon cinnamon

2 cups all-purpose flour

3 tablespoons slivered almonds

1. Heat the oil, anise, and sesame seeds in a medium skillet over medium heat, stirring occasionally, until the oil has absorbed the flavors, about 5 minutes. Let cool.

2. Stir in all but 1 tablespoon of the sugar, and the lemon and orange rinds and juices. Mix the reserved 1 tablespoon of sugar with the cinnamon and set aside. Stir in the flour, a little at a time, until a thick dough forms; work in the last flour additions with your hands, kneading until smooth. Cover with plastic wrap and let rest 30 minutes.

3. Preheat the oven to 375°F.

4. Roll the dough between 2 sheets of plastic wrap to ¼-inch thickness. Cut with a 2-inch round cookie cutter and arrange 2 inches apart on ungreased baking sheets. Decorate with the almond slivers, pressing them in so they adhere, and sprinkle with the cinnamon-sugar mixture. Bake until just starting to brown along the edges, about 12 minutes. Cool 5 minutes on a rack, then remove from the baking sheet and cool completely on the rack.

Per serving (2 cookies): 141 Cal, 6 g Fat, 1 g Sat Fat, 0 mg Chol, 1 mg Sod, 20 g Carb, 1 g Fib, 2 g Prot, 10 mg Calc. **POINTS: 3.**

SMART TIP

Refrigerate these cookies in an airtight container; they'll stay fresh for about six days. The cookies can also be frozen for up to three months.

Tuna Crostini

MAKES 8 SERVINGS

Use a dark Mediterranean olive (niçoise could be substituted for kalamata), but make sure to choose a variety packed in vinegar rather than in oil to save on fat grams.

¾ pound tuna steak
Juice of 1 lemon
1 teaspoon anchovy paste
¼ teaspoon freshly ground pepper
1 plum tomato, chopped
4 scallions, thinly sliced
6 kalamata olives, pitted and chopped
2 tablespoons chopped fresh flat-leaf parsley
8 slices Italian bread, halved crosswise

Easy Elegance
MENU

Tuna Crostini

Shellfish in Endive

Cornish Hens in Apricot Sauce

Roasted Brussels Sprouts *

Rice Pilaf *

Pineapple and Orange Sorbet

Orange Madeleines

No recipe

1. Preheat the broiler. Broil the tuna 4 inches from heat until just opaque in the center, about 5 minutes on each side.
2. Combine the lemon juice, anchovy paste, and pepper in a large bowl. Flake in the tuna, then add the tomato, scallions, olives, and parsley; toss to combine. Mound onto the bread.

Per serving (1 crostini with about 2 teaspoons tuna mixture): 103 Cal, 2 g Fat, 0 g Sat Fat, 1 mg Chol, 227 mg Sod, 18 g Carb, 2 g Fib, 4 g Prot, 47 mg Calc.
POINTS: 2.

SMART TIP
For a smokier flavor, grill the tuna on a ridged grill pan over medium-high heat.

SPECIAL OCCASION NIBBLERS

These simple but sophisticated touches will help make any party memorable:

Whip up a colorful Roasted Red Pepper–Pesto Dip in seconds and serve with peeled, cooked shrimp from the supermarket. Here's how: Puree a 7-ounce jar of well-drained roasted red bell peppers with 1 garlic clove and 1 tablespoon of extra-virgin olive oil; transfer to a serving bowl. Dollop store-bought pesto in dime-size drops on top, swirl lightly.

Create an intensely flavored, all-purpose condiment from inexpensive balsamic vinegar to add a deep, caramelized character to roasted meats, poultry, salads, gravies, even fresh fruit or low-fat vanilla ice cream. Start with 1½ cups of balsamic vinegar, 1 tablespoon firmly packed light brown sugar, and 2 teaspoons light molasses; bring to a boil and cook, stirring frequently, until reduced to ⅔ cup. Play restaurant chef and drizzle it dramatically on a serving plate before topping with an entrée, salad, or fruit. The syrup will last in the fridge up to five days or the freezer up to six months (freeze it in an ice-cube tray and store the cubes in a zip-close freezer bag).

Cornish Hens with Apricot Sauce

MAKES 8 SERVINGS

Serve this with rice pilaf or risotto and simple vegetables, such as roasted Brussels sprouts or sautéed green beans. If you're entertaining, leave the birds whole for a more dramatic presentation. Roast whole birds at 350°F for about one hour (an instant-read thermometer inserted in the thigh should register 180°F).

1 cup orange juice
½ cup + 4 tablespoons coffee liqueur
½ cup apricot preserves
4 tablespoons balsamic vinegar
4 tablespoons Dijon mustard
4 (1½-pound) Cornish hens, quartered

1. Preheat the oven to 450°F. Combine the orange juice, liqueur, and preserves in a small saucepan; bring to a boil. Cook, stirring, until the preserves melt, 1–2 minutes. Reduce the heat and simmer until syrupy, about 4 minutes. Remove from the heat and stir in the vinegar and mustard. Transfer ¼ cup of the sauce to a small bowl.

2. Gently lift the skin from the meat on each hen; brush 1 tablespoon of the sauce from the bowl under the skin of each. Place the hens in a single layer in a roasting pan. Roast until cooked through, about 25 minutes.

3. Just before serving, bring the sauce back to a boil. Place 2 pieces of hen on each of 8 plates; spoon the sauce over each.

Per serving (½ Cornish hen with about 2 tablespoons sauce): 296 Cal, 5 g Fat, 1 g Sat Fat, 103 mg Chol, 279 mg Sod, 30 g Carb, 0 g Fib, 24 g Prot, 34 mg Calc. **POINTS: 6.**

SMART TIP

For a more traditional and slightly sweeter sauce, use ruby port instead of coffee liqueur.

Shellfish in Endive

MAKES 6 SERVINGS

This filling is a modern-day seviche, since the seafood is lightly cooked for safety.

½ red bell pepper, seeded and diced
2 scallions, thinly sliced
1 tablespoon chopped fresh cilantro
⅛ teaspoon crushed red pepper
½ cup dry white wine
1 bay leaf
1 cup water
¼ pound shrimp, peeled, deveined, and diced
¼ pound bay scallops
¼ teaspoon salt
Juice of 2 limes
12 large Belgian endive leaves

1. Combine the bell pepper, scallions, cilantro, and crushed red pepper in a bowl. Set aside.
2. Combine the wine, bay leaf, and the water in a medium saucepan; boil 3 minutes. Reduce the heat and add the shrimp and scallops; simmer until the shrimp turn bright pink, about 1 minute. Drain, discarding the bay leaf, and add the seafood to the pepper mixture. Stir in the salt, then mix in the lime juice. Spoon into the endive leaves.

Per serving (2 endive leaves with 3 tablespoons filling each): 78 Cal, 1 g Fat, 0 g Sat Fat, 35 mg Chol, 169 mg Sod, 7 g Carb, 3 g Fib, 8 g Prot, 53 mg Calc. **POINTS: 1.**

SMART TIP

Feel free to vary the seafood with whatever looks best at your fish market. Try such alternatives or additions as calamari rings (not tentacles) or chunks of red snapper or sole.

Pineapple and Orange Sorbet

MAKES 8 SERVINGS

Even if you usually shun canned fruit, you must try this dessert. Canned fruit makes this recipe almost criminally easy, and you'd never guess you're not eating the freshest fruits. When pureed, the pineapple takes on a pale, off-white hue evocative of cream-laden sherbet.

1 (20-ounce) can crushed pineapple in heavy syrup, frozen
1 (8-ounce) can mandarin oranges in light syrup, frozen
¼ cup packed light brown sugar
¼ cup golden rum

Open the cans on both ends and push the frozen fruit onto a cutting board. Cut into quarters, then transfer to a food processor and pulse about 20 times to break up. Pulse in the brown sugar. With the machine running, drizzle in the rum; process until smooth, about 20 seconds. Spoon the sorbet into parfait glasses.

Per serving (about ½ cup): 123 Cal, 0 g Fat, 0 g Sat Fat, 0 mg Chol, 5 mg Sod, 28 g Carb, 1 g Fib, 0 g Prot, 19 mg Calc. **POINTS: 2.**

SMART TIP

For a more intense tropical flavor, substitute dark rum instead of the golden variety.

Orange Madeleines

MAKES 12 SERVINGS

Madeleines are little shell-shaped cakes, crisp around the edges and spongy inside. They are baked in special madeleine molds with scallop-shell-shaped indentations—which are available at most cookware stores.

¼ cup fat-free egg substitute

¼ cup + 2 tablespoons confectioners' sugar

2 tablespoons unsalted butter, melted

1 teaspoon orange liqueur

3 tablespoons all-purpose flour

1 teaspoon grated orange rind

1 tablespoon chopped bittersweet chocolate

1. Preheat the oven to 350°F. Spray a 12-shell madeleine mold with nonstick cooking spray.

2. Whisk the egg substitute in a large bowl until frothy. Whisk in the confectioners' sugar, butter, and liqueur, then stir in the flour and orange rind. Spoon 1 tablespoon of the batter into each shell of the madeleine mold. Bake until golden brown, 11–12 minutes. Cool in the mold on a wire rack 1 minute, then remove the madeleines from the mold and cool completely on the rack.

3. Put the chocolate into a microwavable bowl. Microwave at 50 percent power about 1½ minutes, stirring every 30 seconds, until melted. Using a small spoon, drizzle chocolate over the cooled madeleines.

Per serving (1 cake): 62 Cal, 2 g Fat, 1 g Sat Fat, 5 mg Chol, 10 mg Sod, 9 g Carb, 0 g Fib, 1 g Prot, 4 mg Calc. **POINTS: 1.**

SMART TIP

If you don't have mandeleine molds handy, use mini-muffin tins instead.

Shrimp Chutney

MAKES 16 SERVINGS

Slightly sweet and spicy with ginger and lemon, shrimp chutney is a great topping for toasted French bread rounds, crackers (garnish each with a parsley leaf and a thin triangle of radish), or our Savory Biscotti. Spoon it onto the bottom of endive leaves, then arrange the filled leaves on a large, round platter in a spiral around a center of leafy-topped radishes. You can also roll spoonfuls of chutney in Boston lettuce leaves, spoon it into hollowed-out cherry tomatoes or dollop a bit on cucumber rounds.

½ pound large shrimp, peeled and deveined

¼ pound sea scallops

½ small garlic clove, finely chopped

¼ teaspoon salt

1 teaspoon olive oil

2 tablespoons fresh lemon juice

2 tablespoons mango (Major Grey's) chutney

2 tablespoons fat-free mayonnaise

Freshly ground pepper, to taste

2 teaspoons finely chopped red onion

½ teaspoon grated peeled fresh ginger

¼ teaspoon grated lemon rind

Thanksgiving Dinner
MENU

Shrimp Chutney

Savory Biscotti

Romaine, Apple, and Radish Salad with Cider Dressing

Corn Bread–Stuffed Turkey Breast with a Spice Crust

Green Beans with Lemon and Garlic

Parsnip Mashed Potatoes

Pumpkin Torte

1. Toss the shrimp and scallops with the garlic and salt in a large bowl.

2. Heat a large nonstick skillet over high heat, 1 minute. Swirl in the oil, then add the shrimp and scallops in a single layer. Cook, turning once, until golden brown on both sides, 1½–2 minutes. Add the lemon juice and cook, stirring, until almost dry; let cool.

3. Put the cooled shrimp mixture, the chutney, mayonnaise, and pepper in a food processor or blender; pulse until finely chopped. Transfer to a bowl and stir in the onion, ginger, and lemon rind. Cover and refrigerate up to 8 hours to blend the flavors.

Per serving (2 tablespoons): 39 Cal, 2 g Fat, 0 g Sat Fat, 21 mg Chol, 75 mg Sod, 2 g Carb, 0 g Fib, 4 g Prot, 9 mg Calc. **POINTS: 1.**

121

SMART TIP

To make the chutney the day before serving, prepare up to pulsing the shrimp mixture in the food processor in Step 3. Transfer the mixture to a small airtight container and refrigerate overnight. Stir in the onion, ginger, and lemon rind just before serving.

Savory Biscotti

MAKES 18 BISCOTTI

For a fresh take on biscotti, make them savory—not sweet—and serve them before the meal. You can make them as spicy as you like, using this basic recipe as a starting point for your own inventions. Try using toasted cumin seeds instead of the fennel seeds. Or, omit the cayenne and replace the fennel with coarsely ground tricolor peppercorns. Use extra-virgin olive oil in place of olive oil for a more intense, savory flavor.

2 tablespoons olive oil

1 tablespoon unsalted butter, melted

3 garlic cloves, finely chopped

2 teaspoons fennel seeds, crushed

½ teaspoon curry powder

2 cups all-purpose flour

2 tablespoons yellow cornmeal

1½ teaspoons baking powder

2 teaspoons sugar

1 teaspoon salt

¼ teaspoon cayenne

2 egg whites

1 large egg

1. Preheat the oven to 350°F.

2. Stir the oil, butter, garlic, fennel seeds, and curry powder in a medium microwavable bowl. Microwave on High until aromatic, 10–35 seconds. Let cool.

3. Whisk the flour, cornmeal, baking powder, sugar, salt, and cayenne in a large bowl.

4. Whisk the egg whites and egg into the butter mixture; stir into the flour mixture with a wooden spoon until a stiff dough forms.

5. On a lightly floured surface, roll dough into two 12-inch logs and place 2 inches apart on an ungreased baking sheet. Bake until light golden and firm to the touch, about 25 minutes. Let cool completely. With a serrated knife, slice the logs on a slight angle ¼-inch thick.

6. Arrange the slices flat-side down on the baking sheet. Bake 5–6 minutes, turn, and bake until light golden on both sides, 5–6 minutes more.

Per serving (2 biscotti): 167 Cal, 5 g Fat, 1 g Sat Fat, 27 mg Chol, 345 mg Sod, 25 g Carb, 1 g Fib, 5 g Prot, 27 mg Calc. **POINTS: 4.**

SMART TIP

To crush the fennel seeds, place them on a piece of wax paper, fold over some of the paper to cover, and then press down with a rolling pin. To keep the biscotti crisp and tasty, store them in an airtight container at room temperature for two weeks or up to one month in the freezer. Defrost for 30 minutes at room temperature before serving. You can also refresh slightly stale biscotti by warming them on a baking sheet in a 350°F oven 10 minutes.

Romaine, Apple, and Radish Salad with Cider Dressing

MAKES 8 SERVINGS

Apple cider creates a rich dressing in this salad that pairs the sweetness of apple with the bracing, peppery bite of radishes. Romaine is the green to stand up to both. When cutting the onion, use a very sharp knife to make thin shavings.

1½ cups unsweetened apple cider
1 medium Granny Smith apple, peeled, cored, and sliced
1 teaspoon sugar
¼ medium red onion, very thinly sliced
2 tablespoons cider vinegar
2 tablespoons olive oil
½ small garlic clove, minced
¼ teaspoon salt
2 medium Romaine lettuce heads, cleaned and torn into bite-size pieces
1 large bunch radishes, thinly sliced

1. Bring the cider to a boil in a small saucepan. Lower the heat and simmer until reduced to 3 tablespoons, 20–25 minutes.
2. Spray a large nonstick skillet with nonstick spray and set over medium-high heat. Add the apple slices in a single layer and cook, turning occasionally, until beginning to brown, 7–8 minutes. Sprinkle with the sugar and cook until deep golden brown and tender, 4 minutes. Let cool.
3. Rinse the onion in a sieve under cool running water, 10 seconds. Drain and pat dry with paper towels. In a large bowl, combine the onion, the reduced cider, the vinegar, oil, garlic, and salt. Add the lettuce, cooked apple, and radishes; toss well to coat.

Per serving (1¼ cups): 86 Cal, 4 g Fat, 1 g Sat Fat, 0 mg Chol, 88 mg Sod, 12 g Carb, 3 g Fib, 2 g Prot, 50 mg Calc. **POINTS: 1.**

SMART TIP
The salad can be made up to one day ahead. You can refrigerate the washed and torn greens and sliced radishes in zip-close plastic bags; cover the cooked apple in plastic wrap. Let the apple come to room temperature before adding to the salad. Rinsing the onion with water before slicing helps remove some of its sharpness and brings out its natural sweetness.

Green Beans with Lemon and Garlic

MAKES 8 SERVINGS

This cool salad is a delicious and refreshing addition to any Thanksgiving Day menu. It's also perfect if you're a guest who has been asked to bring a dish. Watch the timing when cooking the green beans—they should be tender, crisp, and bright green (if you cook them longer than seven minutes, their color will fade).

3 pounds green beans, trimmed
2 teaspoons extra-virgin olive oil
3 garlic cloves, minced
Juice and the grated rind of 1 lemon
1 teaspoon salt

1. Fill a large stockpot or Dutch oven with two-thirds water; bring to a boil. Add the beans and cook just until bright green, 6–7 minutes total (don't wait for the water to boil again). Drain in a colander and rinse under cold running water until cool, 1 minute, or plunge into a large bowl filled with ice water. Drain well.

2. In a microwavable cup measure, heat the oil and garlic on High just until aromatic, 10–20 seconds. Stir in the lemon juice, lemon rind, and salt. Toss with the beans to coat. Serve immediately, or chill up to 1 hour before serving.

Per serving (1 cup): 60 Cal, 1 g Fat, 0 g Sat Fat, 0 mg Chol, 299 mg Sod, 12 g Carb, 5 g Fib, 3 g Prot, 56 mg Calc. **POINTS: 0.**

SMART TIP

If you plan to make this dish ahead of time, cook the beans and place them in the refrigerator up to one day ahead in a zip-close plastic bag. Prepare the dressing on the day of serving; you can take the beans and dressing with you in separate containers if you're traveling. Toss the dressing with the beans no more than one hour before serving, because the acid in the dressing will turn the beans a drab, olive color if they're allowed to stand too long.

Parsnip Mashed Potatoes

MAKES 8 SERVINGS

Yukon gold potatoes and parsnips team up for a deliciously different side dish that's easy to make in your food processor.

2½ pounds Yukon gold potatoes, peeled and cubed

1½ pounds parsnips, peeled and sliced ½-inch thick

1 (14½-ounce) can reduced-sodium chicken broth

1½ cups water

1 tablespoon unsalted butter

2 leeks, white part only, cleaned and chopped

1 teaspoon minced fresh thyme, or ½ teaspoon dried

½ cup fat-free half-and-half

1 tablespoon extra-virgin olive oil

¾ teaspoon salt

¼ teaspoon ground white pepper

1. In a stockpot or Dutch oven, bring the potatoes, parsnips, broth, and the water to a boil. Cook, covered, until the vegetables are very tender, about 25 minutes.

2. Meanwhile, melt the butter in a medium nonstick skillet over medium heat. Add the leeks and cook until softened, 5 minutes; add the thyme and cook until tender, 2–3 minutes more. Set aside.

3. Drain the potato-parsnip mixture in a colander set over a bowl, reserving the liquid. Return the vegetables to the same pot and coarsely mash. Transfer to a food processor.

4. Bring ⅔ cup of the cooking liquid and the half-and-half to a simmer in a medium saucepan; stir in the oil, salt, and pepper. With the food processor running, pour the mixture through the feed tube and pulse, stopping to scrape the sides once or twice, until smooth. Transfer to a serving bowl and stir in the leeks.

Per serving (¾ cup): 240 Cal, 1 g Fat, 1 g Sat Fat, 4 mg Chol, 285 mg Sod, 48 g Carb, 6 g Fib, 5 g Prot, 61 mg Calc. **POINTS: 4.**

SMART TIP

This dish can be made up to two days ahead; simply transfer to a microwavable casserole dish, cover, and refrigerate. On the day of serving, let it come to room temperature then microwave on High 6 minutes, stopping to stir every 2 minutes, until piping hot. To wash the leeks, trim off the green stalks and slice the white part in half lengthwise. Then rinse thoroughly under running water, fanning the layers out to remove all the grit.

Corn Bread–Stuffed Turkey Breast with a Spice Crust

MAKES 8 SERVINGS

Turkey breast has never been so succulent. Here, it's rolled around a corn bread stuffing, sealed in a spicy crust, and drizzled with a jus-style gravy for extra moisture. If you can't find deboned turkey breast in your supermarket, the in-store butcher can debone it for you. If you'd like to try it yourself, see below.

SPICE CRUST

- 1 tablespoon chili powder
- 1 teaspoon ground cumin
- 1 teaspoon chopped fresh thyme, or ½ teaspoon dried
- ½ teaspoon salt

STUFFING

- 2 teaspoons unsalted butter
- 1 medium onion, chopped
- 1 large shallot, chopped
- 2 cups cube-style corn bread stuffing mix
- ⅔ cup reduced-sodium chicken broth, hot
- 1 egg white
- 1 tablespoon chopped fresh parsley
- 1 teaspoon chopped fresh thyme, or ¼ teaspoon dried
- ½ teaspoon salt

continued

1. Preheat the oven to 325°F. To prepare the spice crust, combine the chili powder, cumin, thyme, and salt in a small bowl. Set aside.
2. To prepare the stuffing, melt the butter in a medium skillet over medium heat. Add ⅔ cup of the onion and the shallot; cook until lightly browned, 5–6 minutes. Combine the onion mixture with the stuffing mix, hot broth, egg white, parsley, thyme, and salt in a large bowl, tossing until evenly moistened.
3. To assemble the turkey breast, cut five 20-inch pieces of kitchen twine. On a work surface, arrange the breast skin-side down. With a sharp knife, cut horizontally along the tenderloins, opening them up so that the meat can lie flat. Turn the breast over and slip your fingers under the skin to loosen it. Sprinkle 1 teaspoon of the spice mixture under the skin, spreading over the breast. Turn the breast over and spread the stuffing mixture over the surface of the meat, leaving a 1-inch border. Roll the breast up lengthwise around the filling. (Don't worry about creating a spiral of filling—the meat is too dense to roll easily. Instead, aim for a rounded "roast" with the stuffing tucked inside.) One at a time, slip each piece of twine under the breast and tie securely. Close the open ends with small skewers.
4. Toss the remaining onion with 1 teaspoon of the oil in the center of a shallow roasting pan. Place the stuffed breast seam-side down on top of the onion. Brush the breast with the remaining 1 teaspoon oil; sprinkle the top and sides with the remaining spice mix. Roast 1½ hours. Pour ½ cup of the broth over the turkey; cover with a loose tent of foil. Roast, basting every 15 minutes, until an instant-read thermometer inserted

continued

DEBONING A TURKEY BREAST

Place the breast skin-side down on a cutting board. With a sharp knife, cut straight along the rib cage, freeing the meat as you cut away from the bone. The meat will separate easily from the sides. Cut carefully around the large bone at the broad end.

TURKEY BREAST

1 boneless turkey
   breast
   (4¼–4½ pounds,
   or 5½–6 pounds
   bone-in)
2 teaspoons olive oil
1 (14½-ounce) can
   reduced-sodium
   chicken broth
⅓ cup + 1 tablespoon
   apricot preserves
2 teaspoons
   cornstarch
¼ cup dry white wine

into the thickest part of the breast registers 165°F, 30–45 minutes. Remove from the oven and transfer to a cutting board.

5. In a microwavable cup measure, heat ⅓ cup of the apricot preserves on High until melted, 10–20 seconds. Pour over the turkey; cover with a loose tent of foil and let rest 20 minutes.

6. Meanwhile, to prepare the gravy, whisk the cornstarch into the remaining broth in a small bowl. Add to the drippings in the turkey-roasting pan, along with the wine and the remaining 1 tablespoon apricot preserves; place on the stove and bring to a boil. Cook, stirring constantly, until slightly thickened, 2 minutes.

7. To serve, remove the skewers and strings from the roast and slice. Serve with the gravy. Remove the skin before eating.

Per serving (3 ounces turkey with ¾ cup stuffing): 260 Cal, 4 g Fat, 2 g Sat Fat, 145 mg Chol, 730 mg Sod, 26 g Carb, 1 g Fib, 54 g Prot, 55 mg Calc. **POINTS: 5.**

SMART TIP

> Though the turkey is best served the day you cook it, you can make it 1 day ahead. Wrap the completely cooled roast in plastic wrap, then in foil, and refrigerate. To serve, bring the roast to room temperature; unwrap and remove the plastic. Loosely rewrap the roast in the foil and bake in a preheated 350°F oven 15 minutes, just until warmed through.

NEW LIFE FOR THE LEFTOVERS

Savory Biscotti are wonderful served alongside soups and salads. Jazz them up with a sprinkling of shredded low-fat cheddar cheese and a bit of minced pickled jalapeño pepper; heat in the toaster oven just until the cheese melts. Or, top a biscotti with a spoonful of cottage cheese and a roasted bell pepper strip for a satisfying snack.

Shrimp Chutney makes a great sandwich filling when combined with a chopped, hard-cooked egg. Add a Romaine lettuce leaf and serve between toasted pumpernickel bread slices.

Parsnip Mashed Potatoes add substance to vegetable soup; just stir in a few spoonfuls. Turn a stew into something special by pouring it into a casserole dish and topping it with the mashed potatoes; bake until bubbling and browned. Or, spread the mashed potatoes over fish fillets, roll up, sprinkle with a little olive oil and seasoned bread crumbs, and bake until cooked through.

Leftover Turkey makes for a hearty, healthy soup base: Cook onion, carrots, and some thinly sliced cabbage until tender, add some canned chicken broth, drained and rinsed canned white beans, and chopped turkey. Take this basic recipe, stir in canned diced tomatoes in juice and a pinch of oregano, and you've got minestrone. Or, top a low-fat flour tortilla with a little chopped turkey, salsa, and a sprinkle of shredded reduced-fat cheddar cheese. Toast just until the cheese melts.

Pumpkin Torte

MAKES 12 SERVINGS

Delectable and different, this frozen torte is a breeze to prepare. The secret to its rich taste and creamy texture is fat-free half-and-half. Splurge on premium low-fat ice cream or frozen yogurt for great taste.

- 1 (6-ounce) container low-fat vanilla yogurt
- 1 (¼-ounce) envelope unflavored gelatin
- ¼ cup water
- 1 (15-ounce) can pumpkin puree
- 1½ cups fat-free half-and-half
- 1 cup sugar
- 1 teaspoon vanilla extract
- ½ teaspoon cinnamon
- ⅛ teaspoon salt
- 1 pint low-fat vanilla ice cream or frozen yogurt

1. Freeze a 9-inch round springform pan. Drain the yogurt in a coffee filter or cheesecloth-lined strainer; place over a bowl. Let drain 15 minutes. Transfer the drained yogurt to a large bowl; discard the liquid.

2. Meanwhile, sprinkle the gelatin over the water in a microwavable cup measure. Let stand 5 minutes to soften. Microwave on High 10–15 seconds; stir until dissolved. Whisk together the pumpkin, half-and-half, drained yogurt, sugar, dissolved gelatin, vanilla, ¼ teaspoon of the cinnamon, and the salt. Pour into the prepared pan and freeze until set, 2–3 hours.

3. Soften the ice cream in the refrigerator 15 minutes. Stir the ice cream with the remaining ¼ teaspoon cinnamon in a large bowl until blended. Spread over the surface of the pumpkin layer, swirling to resemble icing. Freeze until firm, about 30 minutes.

4. To serve: Let the torte stand at room temperature until slightly softened, 5–10 minutes. Run a knife around the sides of the torte to release it. Cut into wedges and serve immediately.

Per serving (1/12 of the torte): 144 Cal, 1 g Fat, 1 g Sat Fat, 3 mg Chol, 84 mg Sod, 30 g Carb, 1 g Fib, 3 g Prot, 90 mg Calc. **POINTS: 3.**

SMART TIP

You can make the torte up to two days ahead. Cover the top of the pan with foil, crimping tightly to seal, and store in the freezer.

SPICE IT UP!

**Adding spices is
the hottest way
to pump up the flavor,
not the fat,
in your favorite dishes.**

Cumin-Scented Oven Fries

For a little extra crispness, finish cooking the fries under the broiler.

3 baking potatoes (about 2½ pounds), cut into 12 wedges each
1 tablespoon olive oil
2 teaspoons ground cumin
1 teaspoon garlic powder
1 teaspoon paprika
1 teaspoon salt
¼ teaspoon cayenne
⅛ teaspoon cinnamon

1. Preheat the oven to 450°F; lightly spray a jelly-roll pan with nonstick spray.

2. Combine the potatoes and olive oil in one bowl. Combine the cumin, garlic powder, paprika, salt, cayenne, and cinnamon in another bowl. Sprinkle the spice mixture over the potatoes and toss well.

3. Arrange the potatoes in a single layer on the pan. Bake 20 minutes, then turn the potatoes, and bake until crisp and cooked through, 8–10 minutes longer.

Per serving (6 wedges): 191 Cal, 3 g Fat, 0 g Sat Fat, 0 mg Chol, 402 mg Sod, 39 g Carb, 4 g Fib, 4 g Prot, 24 mg Calc. **POINTS: 3.**

SMART TIP

For a super-spicy meal, serve our Peruvian-Style Chicken Breasts, page 62, along with the fries.

spice it up!

Eggplant and Peppers with Roasted Chiles

MAKES 8 SERVINGS

🔥 This dish makes an excellent appetizer when served at room temperature on water crackers or slices of toasted French bread. The quick-cooking eggplant—combined with colorful red bell peppers, roasted chiles, and coriander—makes for an impressively exotic offering without a lot of effort. You can also serve it as a side dish for your evening meal. Use finely chopped broccoli or asparagus tips instead of eggplant for a delightful variation.

1 tablespoon vegetable oil
1 tablespoon yellow split peas
1 teaspoon coriander seeds
2–3 dried red chiles
1 small (½-pound) eggplant, cut into matchstick-size strips
1 medium red bell pepper, seeded and cut into matchstick-size strips
½ cup warm water
2 tablespoons finely chopped fresh cilantro
Juice of 1 lime
1 teaspoon salt
32 water crackers

1. Heat a wok or large nonstick skillet over medium–high heat. Swirl in the oil, then add the peas, coriander, and chiles. Stir-fry until the peas turn golden brown, the coriander seeds darken, and the chiles slightly blacken, about 1 minute. Remove the pea mixture with a slotted spoon and transfer to a heatproof plate; cool. Then grind in a spice grinder or with a mortar and pestle, until the mixture is finely ground.
2. Add the eggplant and bell pepper to the same wok or skillet and stir-fry until the eggplant is partially tender, 2–4 minutes. Stir in the water, cover, and steam, stirring occasionally, until the eggplant is fork-tender, about 2 minutes.
3. Transfer the eggplant mixture to a serving bowl and stir in the ground spice blend, the cilantro, lime juice, and salt. Serve warm or at room temperature, with a heaping tablespoon over each water cracker.

Per serving (4 eggplant-topped crackers): 97 Cal, 3 g Fat, 0 g Sat Fat, 0 mg Chol, 329 mg Sod, 16 g Carb, 2 g Fib, 2 g Prot, 24 mg Calc. **POINTS: 2.**

SMART TIP
When roasting dried chiles, make sure your kitchen is well ventilated, as the volatile oils in the chiles will become more potent and pungent as they cook.

133

Curried Squash Stew

MAKES 4 SERVINGS

This luscious vegetarian dish with fresh ginger, cumin, and coriander is thickened with millet, a grain that resembles couscous when cooked.

1 teaspoon vegetable oil
1 onion, thinly sliced
1½ tablespoons grated peeled fresh ginger
¾ teaspoons ground cumin
¾ teaspoon ground coriander
½ teaspoon ground turmeric
¼ teaspoon hot pepper sauce
½ cup millet
1 (1-pound) acorn squash, peeled and cubed
3 cups water
2 tomatoes, chopped
1 teaspoon salt
¼ cup minced fresh cilantro
2 teaspoons fresh lemon juice

1. Heat a large saucepan or Dutch oven over medium heat. Swirl in the oil, then add the onion and ginger. Cook until the onion is softened, about 5 minutes. Add the cumin, coriander, turmeric, and pepper sauce; cook, stirring frequently, 1 minute.

2. Add the millet to the onion mixture; cook, stirring constantly, until the millet is well coated, 1 minute. Add the squash, water, the tomatoes, and salt; bring to a boil. Reduce the heat, cover, and simmer, stirring occasionally, until the millet is tender, about 30 minutes. Stir in the cilantro and lemon juice.

Per serving (2 cups): 198 Cal, 3 g Fat, 0 Sat Fat, 0 mg Chol, 573 mg Sod, 39 g Carb, 7 g Fib, 5 g Prot, 48 mg Calc. **POINTS: 3.**

SMART TIP
Serve the stew over basmati rice scented with garam masala, the aromatic and peppery spice combination from India.

Portobello-and-Onion Pita Sandwiches

MAKES 4 SERVINGS

These hearty sandwiches stuffed with meaty portobellos are surprisingly low in **POINTS**. The spiced mushroom filling can be cooked up to one day ahead of time and refrigerated, but for the most flavor, let it return to room temperature before assembling the sandwiches.

1 teaspoon olive oil
1 large onion, chopped
½ teaspoon kosher salt
½ teaspoon ground cumin
½ teaspoon ground coriander
⅛ teaspoon cayenne
Freshly ground pepper, to taste
1 garlic clove, minced
1 (14½-ounce) can reduced-sodium vegetable broth
4 large portobello mushrooms, stems removed
2 cups shredded romaine lettuce
1 chopped tomato
⅓ cup feta cheese, crumbled
4 large pitas
¾ cup Tahini Citrus Dressing (recipe follows)

1. Heat a large nonstick skillet over medium-high heat. Swirl in the oil, then add the onion. Cook until lightly browned, 7–8 minutes. Add the salt, cumin, coriander, cayenne, and pepper; cook, stirring, until aromatic, about 30 seconds. Add the garlic and cook until fragrant, 30 seconds. Add the broth and bring to a simmer. Add the mushrooms, stem-side up, spooning some onions and broth into each cap. Cover the skillet and cook 20 minutes; turn the mushrooms and continue cooking, turning every 5 minutes, until the mushrooms are tender, 35–40 minutes. Remove from heat and let cool in the pan to room temperature.

2. Transfer the mushrooms to a cutting board and slice them ¼-inch thick. Return the mushroom slices to the pan and toss them with the onions.

3. Combine the lettuce, tomato, and feta cheese in a bowl. Cut each pita in half, stuffing each half with ¼ cup of the lettuce mixture and ⅓ cup of the mushroom mixture. Drizzle each portion with 1½ tablespoons of the Tahini Citrus Dressing.

Per serving (1 pita half with ¾ cup filling): 299 Cal, 7 g Fat, 3 g Sat Fat, 11 g Chol, 830 mg Sod, 49 g Carb, 5 g Fib, 12 g Prot, 174 mg Calc. **POINTS: 6.**

SMART TIP

Spices like cumin, coriander, and cayenne release their flavor best when gently toasted in a skillet over medium heat. They should be cooked just until they are aromatic; be careful, they burn easily.

Tahini Citrus Dressing

MAKES 8 SERVINGS

This piquant dressing is delicious drizzled over tomatoes, grilled or roasted meats, and poultry, too. You can also serve it as a dipping sauce with your favorite flat bread.

½ medium cucumber, peeled, seeded, and chopped

¼ cup coarsely chopped fresh parsley

¼ cup coarsely chopped fresh mint

¼ cup fresh lemon juice

1 tablespoon roasted sesame tahini

1 garlic clove, minced

⅛ teaspoon kosher salt

Freshly ground pepper, to taste

Combine all the ingredients in a blender and whirl until smooth. Serve at once, or refrigerate in an airtight container for up to 2 days.

Per serving (1½ tablespoons): 16 Cal, 1 g Fat, 0 g Sat Fat, 0 mg Chol, 29 mg Sod, 2 g Carb, 0 g Fib, 1 g Prot, 17 mg Calc. **POINTS: 0.**

SMART TIP

Look for tahini, a creamy paste made from crushed sesame seeds, in the Middle Eastern foods section of your supermarket. Whether you find it in a jar or a can, you can store opened tahini in the refrigerator for up to one year.

136

IT'S ALL ABOUT SPICES

To get the most out of your spices, make sure they're impeccably fresh. Buy spices in small quantities so they won't languish on your shelves for years (most are best used within six months of purchase). For the longest shelf life, buy whole rather than ground spices—cumin, coriander, and fennel seeds; whole cardamom pods, cinnamon sticks, and whole nutmeg. Grind or grate the spices only as you need them (break cinnamon sticks into small pieces before grinding). An electric coffee grinder is ideal for this purpose; just make sure to have one handy that you use only for grinding spices. A curry should never taste of hazelnut French roast!

Freezing or refrigerating spices isn't a good idea—moisture can seep in and affect their flavor and shelf life. Instead, store them in a cool, dark place, where sunlight and heat won't cause the flavors to fade. It also may be wise to consider scrapping that pretty spice rack by the stove.

Yellow Split Peas with Tomatoes

MAKES 4 SERVINGS

🔥 Dals (a generic term for raw lentils and cooked dishes made with legumes) are integral to any Indian meal—vegetarian or not. Try any of your favorite lentils, beans, or peas with the same spices in this recipe, and you'll be amazed by the diverse flavor and texture of each variety.

4 cups water
1 cup yellow split peas, sorted and rinsed
1 tablespoon unsalted butter
5 medium garlic cloves, minced
1 tablespoon coriander seeds, ground
1 teaspoon cumin seeds, ground
2–3 Thai, cayenne, or serrano chiles, seeded and minced (wear gloves when handling to prevent irritation)
1 large tomato, finely chopped
2 tablespoons finely chopped fresh cilantro
1 teaspoon salt
¼ teaspoon ground turmeric

1. Bring the water and peas to a boil in a medium saucepan over medium-high heat; skim off any foam that floats to the surface. Reduce the heat and simmer, partially covered, until the peas are tender, about 25 minutes. Do not drain; the peas should be a little "soupy."

2. Melt the butter in a large nonstick skillet over medium-high heat. Add the garlic, coriander, cumin, and chiles, and cook until the garlic is golden brown and the spices are fragrant, about 1 minute.

3. Stir in the tomato, cilantro, salt, and turmeric and cook, stirring occasionally, until the tomatoes soften and become almost saucy, 2–3 minutes.

4. Stir in the peas and continue simmering, covered, stirring occasionally, until the flavors blend, about 15 minutes.

Per serving (¾ cup): 224 Cal, 4 g Fat, 2 g Sat Fat, 8 mg Chol, 594 mg Sod, 37 g Carb, 13 g Fib, 13 g Prot, 54 mg Calc. **POINTS: 4.**

SMART TIP
Dals freeze well for up to a month and make for a quickly scrumptious, healthy meal when combined with either steamed rice or bread.

weight watchers

Mushroom and Peas with Garam Masala

MAKES 4 SERVINGS

Garam masala is a blend of spices—usually consisting of aromatically roasted spices such as cumin, cardamom, cinnamon, peppercorns, bay leaves, and cloves—that is commonly used in northern Indian households. This mixture is readily available in supermarkets and gourmet grocery stores. If you can't find it, use a good-quality curry powder instead.

- 1 medium yellow onion, coarsely chopped
- 2 (2-inch) pieces fresh ginger, peeled
- 5 medium garlic cloves, peeled
- 1 tablespoon vegetable oil
- 1 large tomato, finely chopped
- 1 teaspoon garam masala
- 1 teaspoon salt
- ¼ teaspoon ground turmeric
- 1 (8-ounce) package cremini or white mushrooms
- 1 cup frozen green peas, thawed
- ½ cup plain nonfat yogurt
- 2 tablespoons finely chopped fresh cilantro

1. Finely chop the onion, ginger, and garlic in a food processor or blender.

2. Heat a large nonstick skillet or saucepan over medium-high heat. Swirl in the oil, then add the onion mixture. Stir-fry until golden brown, 3–4 minutes.

3. Stir in the tomato, garam masala, salt, and turmeric; cook until the tomatoes soften and become almost saucy, about 5 minutes. Add the mushrooms and peas; reduce the heat and cook, covered, stirring occasionally, until the mushrooms are tender, about 15 minutes.

4. Whisk in the yogurt and cilantro and serve at once.

Per serving (¾ cup): 118 Cal, 4 g Fat, 1 g Sat Fat, 1 mg Chol, 641 mg Sod, 17 g Carb, 4 g Fib, 6 g Prot, 91 mg Calc. **POINTS: 2.**

SMART TIP

If you find morels at your farmers' market or gourmet store and don't mind the expense, substitute them for the cremini mushrooms in the recipe—or, if there's a fungi-phobe at your dinner table, use peeled, boiled, and diced potatoes instead.

spice it up!

Pumpkin Risotto

MAKES 4 SERVINGS

A classic in Italian restaurants, pumpkin risotto with a touch of spice is an elegant choice for a special dinner, and surprisingly simple to make. Be sure to have the table set and the rest of the meal ready before you start; you'll need 20 minutes of stirring time at the stove. Serve it right from the pan.

3½ cups low-sodium chicken broth
4 teaspoons olive oil
2 onions, chopped
1 garlic clove, minced
1 cup Arborio rice
1 cup dry white wine
1 cup canned pumpkin puree
¼ cup grated Parmesan cheese
1 tablespoon packed dark brown sugar
¼ teaspoon cinnamon
¼ teaspoon salt
Ground white pepper, to taste
⅛ teaspoon nutmeg

1. Bring the broth to a boil in a saucepan. Reduce the heat and keep at a simmer.

2. Heat a large nonstick saucepan over medium-high heat. Swirl in the oil, and then add the onions and garlic. Cook until softened. Add the rice and cook, stirring, until the outer shell is translucent, about 1 minute.

3. Add the wine and ½ cup of the broth; stir until they are absorbed. Continue to add broth, ½ cup at a time, stirring until it is absorbed before adding more, until the rice is just tender. The cooking time from the first addition of broth should be about 20 minutes. Stir in the pumpkin, cheese, brown sugar, cinnamon, salt, and pepper; heat through. Sprinkle with the nutmeg and serve at once.

Per serving (1¼ cups): 357 Cal, 10 g Fat, 3 g Sat Fat, 8 mg Chol, 439 mg Sod, 48 g Carb, 1 g Fib, 11 g Prot, 187 mg Calc. **POINTS: 8.**

SMART TIP

To make fresh pumpkin puree, chop ¼ pound of peeled pumpkin (butternut squash works well, too) into 1-inch chunks. Boil the pumpkin in 1 cup of water until tender, and then puree the pumpkin with about ½ cup of the cooking liquid in a food processor or blender.

Grilled Spiced Pork with Orange-Lime Glaze and Sugar Snap Peas

MAKES 4 SERVINGS

California is a true melting pot for ethnic foods. It is, in fact, the birthplace of fusion cuisine. This recipe melds Chinese and Mexican ingredients, creating a rather natural partnership, since the two cuisines often overlap in the use of certain herbs and spices. The spicy rub gives the pork great depth of flavor, while the simple glaze, which uses orange marmalade as a shortcut, adds a welcome sweetness.

½ cup orange marmalade

2 tablespoons fresh lime juice

1 teaspoon finely chopped shallot

1½ teaspoons chili powder

1 teaspoon sugar

¾ teaspoon salt

¼ teaspoon five-spice powder

1 (12-ounce) pork tenderloin, trimmed of all visible fat

¾ pound sugar snap peas, trimmed

1½ teaspoons safflower oil

1½ teaspoons rice vinegar

¼ teaspoon grated peeled fresh ginger

Freshly ground pepper, to taste

1. Spray the grill rack with nonstick spray; prepare the grill for medium-hot fire.

2. Bring the marmalade, lime juice, and shallot to a boil in a small saucepan; boil 2 minutes. Allow to cool, then transfer half of the glaze to a small bowl.

3. Blend the chili powder, sugar, ½ teaspoon of the salt, and the five-spice powder in a small bowl. Rub the spice all over the pork. Grill the pork 5 inches from heat, turning and brushing with half of the glaze, until an instant-read thermometer inserted in the center of meat registers 160°F, 20–25 minutes.

4. Meanwhile, cook the sugar snap peas in a saucepan of boiling water until crisp-tender, 2–3 minutes. Rinse under cold water and drain. Toss the sugar snap peas with the oil, vinegar, ginger, the remaining ¼ teaspoon salt, and the pepper.

5. Gently warm the remaining glaze over low heat. Slice the tenderloin, drizzle with the glaze, and serve with the sugar snap peas.

Per serving (3 ounces pork with ½ cup peas): 327 Cal, 7 g Fat, 2 g Sat Fat, 84 mg Chol, 538 mg Sod, 35 g Carb, 4 g Fib, 32 g Prot, 82 mg Calc. **POINTS: 6.**

SMART TIP

Serve jasmine rice as a perfectly flavored accompaniment to the spicy pork.

HERE'S THE RUB

A dry or spice rub is a combination of dry herbs and spices that is rubbed over meat, fish, or chicken to add flavor before cooking. **For a Mexican-style rub,** combine ground cumin, ground coriander, ground cinnamon, oregano, thyme, salt, and freshly ground pepper. Add some brown sugar, chili powder, and dry mustard to create a rub perfect for seasoning grilled meats and chicken.

Yogurt-Marinated Salmon Fillets

MAKES 4 SERVINGS

This tangy marinade with cayenne, coriander, cumin, and turmeric perfectly complements delicate but rich-tasting salmon. For a smokier taste sensation, grill the fish fillets outdoors, over charcoal and mesquite chips.

1 cup plain nonfat yogurt, whisked

½ teaspoon cayenne

6 medium garlic cloves, minced

2 (2-inch) pieces fresh ginger, peeled and minced

2 tablespoons finely chopped fresh cilantro

1 tablespoon coriander seeds, ground

1 teaspoon cumin seeds, ground

1 teaspoon salt

¼ teaspoon ground turmeric

4 (6-ounce) skinless boneless salmon fillets

1. Combine all the ingredients except the salmon fillets in a zip-close plastic bag; mix well. Add the fillets. Squeeze out the air and seal the bag; turn to coat the fillets. Refrigerate, turning the bag occasionally, at least 2 hours or overnight.

2. Spray the broiler rack with nonstick spray; preheat the broiler. Remove the salmon fillets from the marinade and place on a plate, pouring off the excess marinade into a small saucepan.

3. Bring the marinade to a boil over medium-high heat; reduce the heat and simmer, stirring occasionally, 2 minutes. Set aside.

4. Place the fillets on the broiler rack and broil 5 inches from heat, brushing with the reserved marinade once or twice during cooking, until the salmon is crusty-brown and flakes easily with a fork, about 5–7 minutes per side.

Per serving (1 fillet): 268 Cal, 10 g Fat, 3 g Sat Fat, 112 mg Chol, 417 mg Sod, 4 g Carb, 0 g Fib, 38 g Prot, 93 mg Calc. **POINTS: 6.**

SMART TIP

This recipe can easily be halved or doubled, making it ideal for an intimate supper for two or for a larger gathering. You can use halibut or tuna steaks for variation, and the flavors in the marinade also work beautifully with poultry, pork, and even shellfish.

spice it up!

Pork Barbecue

MAKES 4 SERVINGS

Barbecue lovers from coast to coast debate which state has the best barbecue. North Carolina chimes in with this flavorful sauce, infused with vinegar, paprika, freshly ground pepper, cumin, chili powder, and red pepper flakes. Depending on where you are in the state, tomato may be included.

- 3 tablespoons packed dark brown sugar
- 2 teaspoons paprika
- ¾ teaspoon freshly ground pepper
- ½ teaspoon salt
- ¼ teaspoon ground cumin
- ¼ teaspoon chili powder
- 1½ pounds pork tenderloin, trimmed of all visible fat
- 1 teaspoon vegetable oil
- ⅔ cup cider vinegar
- ⅓ cup water
- ¼ cup ketchup
- 2 tablespoons minced onion
- 1 garlic clove, minced
- ¼ teaspoon crushed red pepper
- 4 hamburger rolls

1. Preheat the oven to 450°F. Mix 1 tablespoon of the brown sugar, the paprika, ½ teaspoon of the pepper, ¼ teaspoon of the salt, the cumin, and chili powder in a small cup. Place the pork on a piece of wax paper. Sprinkle the spice mixture over the pork, patting the meat to help the spices adhere.

2. Heat a large nonstick skillet over medium-high heat. Swirl in the oil, and then add the pork. Cook, turning occasionally, until well browned, about 5 minutes. Transfer the pork to a shallow roasting pan. Roast until an instant-read thermometer inserted in the center of meat registers 160°F, about 15 minutes. Let stand 10 minutes.

3. Meanwhile, combine the remaining 2 tablespoons brown sugar, ¼ teaspoon each pepper and salt, the vinegar, water, ketchup, onion, garlic, and crushed red pepper in a saucepan; bring to a boil. Reduce the heat slightly and boil until reduced to ¾ cup, about 15 minutes.

4. Thinly slice the pork. Toss the pork and ¼ cup of the sauce in a large bowl. Serve on the rolls with the remaining sauce on the side.

Per serving (1 roll with 1 cup sliced pork): 411 Cal, 10 g Fat, 3 g Sat Fat, 101 mg Chol, 808 mg Sod, 39 g Carb, 2 g Fib, 40 g Prot, 89 mg Calc. **POINTS: 9.**

SMART TIP

For do-ahead ease, marinate the pork with the spice mixture and prepare the sauce 1 day ahead then cover each separately and refrigerate overnight.

144

PASTA
PLUS

**Nuts about noodles?
We've got terrific ideas
for every shape
and size of them.**

Mediterranean Spaghetti with Fresh Tuna

MAKES 2 SERVINGS

This pasta dish highlights the best of the Mediterranean diet—fresh fish and olive oil. Pair your meal with a 4-ounce glass of red wine (2 **POINTS**)—another mainstay of the Mediterranean diet—and drink to good health.

- 3 ounces thin spaghetti
- 2 teaspoons olive oil
- 2 (4-ounce) tuna steaks
- 4 canned anchovy fillets, rinsed and mashed
- 2 garlic cloves, minced
- ⅛ teaspoon crushed red pepper
- 2 cups low-sodium, canned plum tomatoes
- 2 tablespoons chopped fresh oregano
- 2 tablespoons chopped fresh basil

1. Cook the spaghetti according to package directions. Drain and keep warm.

2. Heat a large nonstick skillet over medium-high heat. Swirl in the oil, then add the tuna. Cook until the tuna is seared on one side; turn and cook until second side is seared, 1 minute longer.

3. Add the anchovies, garlic, and crushed red pepper to skillet; cook, stirring constantly until the anchovies dissolve, 30 seconds. Stir in the tomatoes and oregano; increase the heat to high. Cook, turning the tuna once, until it flakes easily when tested with a fork, 5 minutes.

4. With a fork, break the tuna into chunks; stir to mix with the tomato mixture. Add the reserved cooked spaghetti; toss to combine. Transfer the mixture to a plate and sprinkle with the basil.

Per serving: 436 Cal, 12 g Fat, 2 g Sat Fat, 47 mg Chol, 373 mg Sod, 44 g Carb, 3 g Fib, 37 g Prot, 129 mg Calc. **POINTS: 9.**

SMART TIP

For variety, use spinach pasta or you can substitute another firm-flesh fish for the tuna, such as swordfish.

Pasta with Autumn Vegetables

MAKES 4 SERVINGS

Delicate capellini, or angel-hair pasta, is best served with broths, not sauces. Here, we use a topper of spice-infused broth with butternut squash and sweet vegetables.

- 1 parsnip, cut into matchstick-size pieces
- 1⅓ cups matchstick-size pieces butternut squash
- 2 teaspoons olive oil
- 1 cup fresh or thawed frozen corn kernels
- 1 small leek, cleaned and sliced
- ¾ cup low-sodium chicken broth
- ¾ teaspoon ground cumin
- ½ teaspoon ground coriander
- ½ pound capellini
- 1½ cups fresh or thawed frozen sugar snap peas
- 2 teaspoons grated Parmesan cheese

1. Place a heavy baking sheet into the oven and preheat the oven to 400°F. Combine the parsnip and squash in a bowl and toss with 1½ teaspoons of the oil. Toss the corn with the remaining ½ teaspoon oil in another bowl. Arrange the parsnips and squash on the baking sheet and roast 5 minutes. Add the corn and roast for another 5 minutes. Stir and roast until vegetables are lightly browned, about 5 minutes longer. Transfer to a bowl.

2. Spray a medium nonstick skillet with nonstick spray and set over high heat. Add the leek and cook until lightly browned, 4–5 minutes. Stir in the broth, cumin, and coriander. Cook, stirring, 3 minutes; remove from the heat and set aside.

3. Bring a large pot of water to a boil. Add the capellini and cook 2 minutes, and then add the sugar snap peas and cook 30 seconds longer. Drain and combine with the vegetables in the bowl. Add the leek sauce and toss to coat. Sprinkle with the cheese and serve at once.

Per serving (2¼ cups): 318 Cal, 5 g Fat, 1 Sat Fat, 2 mg Chol, 417 mg Sod, 60 g Carb, 7 g Fib, 12 g Prot, 106 mg Calc. **POINTS: 6.**

SMART TIP

Roast the vegetables ahead if you like; let them stand covered at room temperature up to two hours.

MAKING THE CUT

The shell of some winter squashes can be tough to open. Here's our method: Steady the squash on a damp towel. Place a sharp, heavy knife, tip-first, into the squash, then pull down slowly on the blade. Pull it out and start again, a little farther down, repeating as necessary, until the squash splits (if you have one, use a mallet to speed the process). Or, soften the squash in the microwave first: Pierce it in several places with a fork, then microwave on High, stopping to turn the squash occasionally until it's soft enough to pierce fairly easily, 5–8 minutes, depending on the size of the squash.

Penne with Mushrooms, Italian Sausage, and Broccoli

MAKES 4 SERVINGS

⌐ This dish is a fast one-pot meal for a busy weeknight and a great showcase for the meatiness of mushrooms; they help stretch the turkey sausage, so you only need a little meat. Omit the cheese, if you like; the dish is still plenty hearty without it.

¼ pound hot Italian-style turkey sausage, any casings removed

1 (10-ounce) package white mushrooms, cleaned and sliced

1 garlic clove, minced

4 cups cooked broccoli florets

4 cups cooked, drained penne (10 ounces dried)

¾ cup reduced-sodium chicken broth

1 tablespoon fresh lemon juice

Crushed red pepper, to taste (optional)

¼ cup grated Parmesan cheese

1. Crumble the turkey sausage meat into a large nonstick skillet and cook until golden brown. Remove the sausage with a slotted spoon and let drain on a paper towel–lined heatproof plate. Pour off and discard any fat in the skillet. Add the mushrooms and cook until they are golden brown and all the juices have evaporated, about 10 minutes.

2. Add the garlic and cook, stirring until fragrant, about 30 seconds. Add the broccoli and the drained sausage; cook until warmed through. Stir in the penne, broth, lemon juice, and the crushed red pepper (if using); cook just until heated through. Serve sprinkled with cheese.

Per serving (2 cups): 412 Cal, 7 g Fat, 2 g Sat Fat, 26 mg Chol, 787 mg Sod, 65 g Carb, 6 g Fib, 23 g Prot, 162 mg Calc. *POINTS: 8.*

SMART TIP

Slash prep work by using thawed frozen broccoli in place of fresh. Or, try substituting chopped broccoli rabe, an earthy Italian green; its slight bitterness helps cut through the richness of the turkey sausage. You can find broccoli rabe in better supermarkets and farmers' markets. Make this dish 1 day ahead and refrigerate in an airtight container; just drain off the broth and reserve it separately (otherwise the pasta will absorb the liquid and become mushy). To reheat, just combine the pasta mixture and broth in a 2-quart casserole dish, cover, and bake in a 350°F oven until warmed through, about 15–20 minutes.

Orange Vegetable Couscous

MAKES 4 SERVINGS

Couscous isn't a grain but a pasta—the fastest cooking kind there is. Like all dried pastas, it is made from durum wheat, and precooked and dried before packaging.

- **4** teaspoons olive oil
- **1** medium zucchini, chopped
- **1** medium yellow squash, chopped
- **1** onion, chopped
- **2** garlic cloves, minced
- **¾** teaspoon salt
- **1** (15-ounce) can chickpeas (garbanzo beans), rinsed and drained
- **¾** cup orange juice
- **½** cup water
- **½** teaspoon dried oregano
- **⅛** teaspoon cayenne
- **1** cup couscous
- **1** pint cherry tomatoes, halved
- **¼** cup thinly sliced fresh basil

1. Heat a large saucepan over medium-high heat. Swirl in 2 teaspoons of the oil, then add the zucchini, squash, onion, garlic, and ¼ teaspoon of the salt. Cook, stirring occasionally, until the vegetables are softened, 4–5 minutes. Add the chickpeas and cook 2 minutes longer. Transfer to a large bowl.

2. Return the pan to the heat and add the remaining 2 teaspoons oil, ½ teaspoon salt, the orange juice, water, oregano, and cayenne; bring to a boil. Stir in the couscous, cover, and remove from the heat; let stand 5 minutes. Transfer the couscous to the bowl with the vegetables. Add the tomatoes and basil and toss to combine.

Per serving (1½ cups): 399 Cal, 7 g Fat, 1 g Sat Fat, 0 mg Chol, 629 mg Sod, 71 g Carb, 9 g Fib, 15 g Prot, 85 mg Calc. **POINTS: 8.**

SMART TIP
Serve the couscous immediately or at room temperature.

Classic Macaroni Salad

MAKES 6 SERVINGS

Macaroni salad is a picnic or barbecue must. To jazz up this old favorite, try using spirals, bow ties, or penne instead of elbow macaroni.

- 6 ounces elbow macaroni
- 5 sweet gherkin pickles, chopped
- 1 red bell pepper, seeded and chopped
- 1 green bell pepper, seeded and chopped
- 1 celery stalk, chopped
- 2 scallions, chopped
- ¾ cup reduced-fat mayonnaise
- 2 tablespoons cider vinegar
- 2 tablespoons Dijon mustard

1. Cook the macaroni according to package directions. Drain and rinse with cold water; transfer to a large bowl. Add the pickles, red and green bell peppers, celery, and scallions.
2. In a small bowl, combine the mayonnaise, vinegar, and mustard. Pour over the macaroni mixture and toss well.

Per serving (1 cup): 227 Cal, 11 g Fat, 2 g Sat Fat, 10 mg Chol, 350 mg Sod, 29 g Carb, 2 g Fib, 4 g Prot, 20 mg Calc. **POINTS: 5.**

SMART TIP

For an added zing, just stir in a few drops of your favorite hot sauce to the dressing. If you have any on hand, add some fresh herbs such as chopped basil or thyme to put your own spin on this classic dish.

Fusilli with Fennel and Peppers

MAKES 1 SERVING

The sweet taste of fennel makes the perfect foil to tangy goat cheese in this terrific pasta dinner for one. For a stronger flavor burst, replace the goat cheese with an equal amount of feta or blue cheese.

1½ ounces fusilli (spiral-shaped pasta)
1 teaspoon olive oil
1½ cups julienned fennel
½ cup low-sodium chicken broth
½ medium red bell pepper, seeded and thinly sliced
1 tablespoon chopped fresh sage, thyme, rosemary, or any combination
1 garlic clove, minced
1½ ounces mild goat cheese, crumbled
1 tablespoon chopped fresh flat-leaf parsley
Freshly ground pepper, to taste

1. Cook the fusilli according to package directions; drain and keep warm.

2. Meanwhile, heat a medium nonstick skillet over medium heat. Swirl in the oil, then add the fennel. Cook, stirring frequently, until the fennel begins to soften, about 3 minutes. Stir in the broth; increase the heat to high. Cook, stirring occasionally, until the fennel is tender.

3. Add the bell pepper, herbs, and garlic to the fennel mixture; reduce the heat to medium. Cook, stirring occasionally, until the vegetables are tender.

4. Add the cooked fusilli to the vegetable mixture; toss to combine. Add the cheese, parsley, and pepper; toss again to combine.

Per serving: 426 Cal, 19 g Fat, 10 g Sat Fat, 34 mg Chol, 415 mg Sod, 47 g Carb, 4 g Fib, 19 g Prot, 236 mg Calc. **POINTS: 9.**

SMART TIP

You can refrigerate any leftover uncooked fennel tightly wrapped in an airtight plastic bag for up to five days.

Gnocchi with Pumpkin Sauce

MAKES 4 SERVINGS

Gnocchi (NYOK-kee), Italian for dumplings, are nuggets of dough usually made from potatoes and flour. They work best with well-seasoned, hearty sauces, like this autumn-inspired one. Find them fresh or frozen in supermarkets and Italian import stores.

4 teaspoons olive oil
1 (2-pound) pumpkin or butternut squash, peeled, halved, seeded, and chopped
3 shallots, minced
1 garlic clove, minced
2 cups low-sodium chicken broth
1 tablespoon chopped fresh thyme, or
  1 teaspoon dried
1 tablespoon minced fresh sage, or
  1 teaspoon dried and crumbled
¼ teaspoon ground white pepper
1 pound fresh or frozen potato gnocchi
4 teaspoons grated Parmesan cheese
1 tablespoon packed light brown sugar
¼ teaspoon ground nutmeg
Fresh sage leaves

1. Heat a large nonstick skillet over medium-high heat. Swirl in the oil, then add the pumpkin, shallots, and garlic. Cook until the shallots begin to turn golden. Add the broth, thyme, sage, and pepper; cook, stirring frequently, until the pumpkin is softened and the liquid is reduced by two-thirds, 15–20 minutes longer.

2. Transfer the sauce into a food processor or blender and puree. Thin with water if needed, 1 tablespoon at a time, until it reaches the desired consistency.

3. Meanwhile, cook the gnocchi in a large pot of boiling water according to the package directions. With a slotted spoon, transfer the gnocchi to a bowl. Pour the sauce over the gnocchi; then sprinkle with the cheese, brown sugar, and nutmeg. Serve garnished with sage leaves.

Per serving (½ cup gnocchi with ¾ cup sauce): 301 Cal, 14 g Fat, 6 g Sat Fat, 25 mg Chol, 487 mg Sod, 39 g Carb, 2 g Fib, 8 g Prot, 109 mg Calc. **POINTS: 7.**

SMART TIP

In a hurry? Substitute 1 cup of canned pumpkin puree for the whole pumpkin. Cook the pumpkin mixture until the flavors blend; no need to puree.

Spaghetti with Baked Summer Tomatoes

Make less pasta if you prefer, and store the remaining sauce in the fridge for up to four days, or freeze it. The recipe easily doubles or even triples; freeze the extra sauce and tomatoes for a taste of summer in the depths of December (if you can wait that long).

12 medium-to-large firm ripe tomatoes
½ teaspoon salt
Freshly ground pepper, to taste
½ cup chopped fresh parsley
2 tablespoons extra-virgin olive oil
3–6 garlic cloves, minced
1½ pounds spaghetti
1 tablespoon unsalted butter
½ cup chopped fresh basil
½ cup grated Asiago or Parmesan cheese

1. Preheat the oven to 425°F. Spray a jelly-roll pan with nonstick spray. Halve the tomatoes widthwise and place cut-side up in the pan. Sprinkle with the salt and pepper.

2. Combine ⅓ cup of the parsley with the oil and garlic in a small bowl; spread over the tops of the tomatoes. Bake until the tomatoes are lightly browned, about 1 hour. If the tomato skins are tough, remove them from 12 of the tomato halves with your fingers as soon as they are cool enough to handle (they should easily slip off).

3. Cook the spaghetti according to package directions; drain and keep warm.

4. Meanwhile, in a small skillet, melt the butter over medium heat, stirring gently, until it begins to turn golden brown and fragrant, about 1 minute. Immediately remove from the heat, stir to cool slightly, and pour into a warm serving bowl. Add the 12 skinned baked tomato halves, the basil, and the remaining parsley; coarsely mash. Add the cooked spaghetti and the cheese; gently toss to combine. Top with the remaining tomato halves and drizzle with the pan juices. Serve hot or at room temperature.

Per serving (1 cup spaghetti with ¼ cup sauce, plus 1½ tomato halves): 402 Cal, 8 g Fat, 3 g Sat Fat, 8 mg Chol, 252 mg Sod, 69 g Carb, 5 g Fib, 14 g Prot, 111 mg Calc. **POINTS: 8.**

SMART TIP

If you plan to freeze some of the sauce, don't add the reserved parsley or the basil in that portion. Store the sauce and the tomato halves in separate zip-close freezer bags, squeezing out the air. To serve later, thaw the sauce and tomatoes overnight in the refrigerator and reheat them separately in the microwave (this will preserve the summer-fresh flavor better than stovetop cooking). Sprinkle in the freshly chopped basil and parsley as directed in Step 4 of the recipe.

Oyster Mushroom Consommé with Cheese Tortellini

MAKES 4 SERVINGS

A consommé is a flavorful clear soup. Because of its flavor and low calorie count, it makes an ideal first course, or you can double the portion size and serve it as a main course. It stores well, so prepare plenty. For maximum flavor, don't add the scallions and tarragon until just before serving.

4 cups reduced-sodium vegetable broth

1 cup water

¼ ounce dried porcini mushrooms

½ pound oyster mushrooms, stems removed, chopped into bite-size pieces

½ medium carrot, finely chopped

½ celery stalk, finely chopped

3 medium scallions, thinly sliced

1 teaspoon chopped fresh tarragon

¼ teaspoon kosher salt

⅛ teaspoon cayenne

2 cups cooked cheese tortellini

1. Bring 1 cup of the broth and water to a simmer in a saucepan. Remove from heat and add the porcinis; let soak 30 minutes. Lift the porcinis out of the broth using a slotted spoon; gently squeeze any excess liquid back into the bowl. Finely chop the porcinis.

2. Strain the broth through a fine-mesh strainer into a clean saucepan; add remaining broth, and bring it to a simmer. Add the oyster and porcini mushrooms; simmer, uncovered, until the mushrooms are almost tender, about 20 minutes. Add the carrot and celery, and cook until the vegetables are tender, about 8 minutes. Add the scallions, tarragon, salt, and cayenne; stir and remove from heat.

3. Divide the cooked tortellini into 4 soup bowls and ladle the consommé over them; serve immediately.

Per serving (1¼ cups): 176 Cal, 6 g Fat, 3 g Sat Fat, 80 mg Chol, 401 mg Sod, 24 g Carb, 2 g Fib, 8 g Prot, 93 mg Calc. **POINTS: 4.**

SMART TIP

If you're serving consommé to your guests and want it to be perfectly clear, pour it through a strainer lined with a damp paper towel. It will collect those extra-fine particles that tend to make a consommé cloudy.

155

Linguine Vegetable Salad

MAKES 1 SERVING

This fresh-tasting pasta salad is a showcase for summer vegetables; feel free to vary the pasta shapes and the produce, depending on what looks good at the farmers' market. It's delicious warm or chilled; make the pasta a day or two ahead or in the cool of the morning, rinse it in a colander (to prevent sticking), and chill until you need it. By all means, add a grating of fresh Parmesan, if you like (2 teaspoons equal 1 **POINT**).

1½ ounces linguine, cooked and drained (about ¾ cup)

½ cup snow peas, sliced into thin strips

½ cup thinly sliced zucchini

½ cup drained cooked chickpeas (garbanzo beans)

3 cherry tomatoes, halved

¼ cup chopped scallions

1 tablespoon tomato puree

1 tablespoon fresh lime juice

1 tablespoon water

1 teaspoon red-wine vinegar

½ teaspoon olive oil

1 garlic clove, halved

2 drops hot pepper sauce

1. To prepare the salad, combine the linguine, snow peas, zucchini, chickpeas, and tomato halves in a small bowl; set aside.
2. To prepare the dressing, combine the scallions, tomato puree, lime juice, water, vinegar, oil, garlic, and pepper sauce in a blender or food processor; puree until smooth.
3. Pour the dressing over the salad; toss to coat.

Per serving: 433 Cal, 6 g Fat, 1 g Sat Fat, 0 mg Chol, 90 mg Sod, 77 g Carb, 9 g Fib, 19 g Prot, 133 mg Calc. **POINTS: 8.**

SMART TIP

The savory dressing is great on any type of pasta-based salad, including couscous and rice-shaped orzo; double the recipe if you like. But what to do with the leftover tomato puree? Freeze it in an ice cube tray until firm, then place the frozen cubes in a zip-close bag to use as needed to jazz up soups, sauces, and dressings. They'll stay fresh for up to three months. Thaw the cubes overnight in the fridge when ready to use.

Rigatoni with Sweet Pepper Sauce

MAKES 12 SERVINGS

If you're not feeding a crowd, you'll welcome the delicious leftover sauce, which freezes beautifully and also makes a great topping for pizza. You can also stir a few spoonfuls into a soup or into hot cooked rice or sliced potatoes. If you like, any chunky type of pasta, such as penne or farfalle, can stand in for the rigatoni.

2 tablespoons olive oil
4 garlic cloves, smashed
1 medium sweet onion, coarsely chopped
3 large bell peppers (use a variety of colors), seeded and chopped into ½-inch chunks
1½ pounds (8–10) small tomatoes (try to match bell pepper color)
2 pounds rigatoni
½ cup finely chopped fresh basil
¾ teaspoon salt
Freshly ground pepper, to taste

1. Heat a large nonstick skillet over medium heat. Swirl in the oil, then add the garlic. Cook, stirring, just until fragrant, about 1 minute. Add the onion and cook until softened, about 7 minutes. Add the bell peppers and cook until they begin to blister, 8–10 minutes. Add the tomatoes and simmer until tender, about 20 minutes.

2. Transfer the mixture in batches to a food processor and pulse until coarsely chopped (don't chop too finely; the sauce should have a chunky texture). Return to the skillet and keep warm.

3. Meanwhile, cook the pasta according to package directions. Drain and keep warm.

4. In a large warmed serving bowl, combine the pasta, sauce, basil, salt, and pepper; toss well to coat. Serve hot or at room temperature.

Per serving (about 1¼ cups pasta with ⅓ cup sauce): 336 Cal, 4 g Fat, 1 g Sat Fat, 0 mg Chol, 153 mg Sod, 64 g Carb, 4 g Fib, 11 g Prot, 26 mg Calc. **POINTS: 6.**

SMART TIP

To freeze the sauce, place in a zip-close freezer bag and seal, squeezing out the air. Try using the 1-quart-size bags to freeze the sauce in 2-cup portions; each will make enough to sauce a pound of pasta. To reheat, thaw the sauce overnight in the refrigerator and microwave it in a covered microwavable bowl; this will preserve fresh flavor better than stovetop cooking. (If you can, wait until after thawing and reheating to add the basil, as the herb will lose potency in the freezer.)

weight watchers

SWEETS & BAKED GOODS

Our collection of frosty, fruity delights, cakes, cookies, and bread-basket treats only taste indulgent.

Carrot Tea Bread

MAKES 8 SERVINGS

When you want something sweet in the afternoon, a warmed slice of this carrot-studded bread makes a satisfying snack.

1 cup all-purpose flour
½ cup whole-wheat flour
1½ cups packed dark brown sugar
1½ teaspoons cinnamon
½ teaspoon salt
½ teaspoon baking soda
¼ teaspoon baking powder
¼ teaspoon nutmeg
Pinch ground cloves
1 large egg
2 egg whites
4 teaspoons vegetable oil
2¾ cups unsweetened applesauce
½ cup sliced cooked carrots
½ cup dried currants

1. Preheat the oven to 400°F; spray two 5 x 3-inch nonstick loaf pans with nonstick cooking spray.

2. In a large strainer, combine the all-purpose flour, whole-wheat flour, brown sugar, cinnamon, salt, baking soda, baking powder, nutmeg, and cloves; sift by shaking into a medium bowl.

3. In a food processor, combine the egg and egg whites until frothy, 30 seconds. With the machine running, gradually drizzle in the oil; process 10 seconds longer. Add ¾ cup of the applesauce and the carrots; process until smooth. Add the flour mixture; pulse 2 times to blend. Add the currants; pulse 4 times to chop.

4. Divide the batter between the loaf pans. Bake until a toothpick inserted in the center comes out clean, 35–40 minutes. Remove from the pan and cool completely on a rack. Serve with the remaining 2 cups applesauce on the side.

Per serving (1¼-inch-thick slice with ¼ cup applesauce): 237 Cal, 4 g Fat, 1 g Sat Fat, 27 mg Chol, 267 mg Sod, 48 g Carb, 3 g Fib, 5 g Prot, 48 mg Calc. **POINTS: 4.**

SMART TIP

If you only have light brown sugar on hand, that's fine. The bread will just have slightly less molasses flavor.

sweets & baked goods

Pumpkin-Apple Bread

MAKES 10 SERVINGS

When you're short on time, bake this bread in a muffin tin instead of a loaf pan. Start testing for doneness after 15 to 20 minutes.

2 cups all-purpose flour
¼ cup granulated sugar
1 teaspoon baking powder
½ teaspoon baking soda
½ teaspoon salt
½ teaspoon cinnamon
1 large egg
1 cup low-fat buttermilk
1 apple, peeled, cored, and grated
½ cup canned pumpkin puree
1 teaspoon confectioners' sugar

1. Preheat the oven to 350°F; spray a 9 x 5-inch loaf pan with nonstick cooking spray.

2. In a large bowl, combine the flour, granulated sugar, baking powder, baking soda, salt, and cinnamon. In a small bowl, beat the egg; add the buttermilk, apple, and pumpkin. Pour over the flour mixture; stir just until blended (do not overmix).

3. Spoon into the pan. Bake until a toothpick inserted in the center comes out clean, 1–1¼ hours. Cool in the pan on a rack 10 minutes; remove from the pan and cool completely on the rack. Dust with the confectioners' sugar and serve.

Per serving (¹⁄₁₀ of bread): 137 Cal, 1 g Fat, 0 g Sat Fat, 22 mg Chol, 243 mg Sod, 28 g Carb, 1 g Fib, 4 g Prot, 57 mg Calc. **POINTS: 3.**

SMART TIP

Vary the taste of the bread with the variety of apple— Golden Delicious or Fuji for sweetness or Granny Smith for flavor that's a bit more tart.

COOL IT!

Preserve the freshness of homemade bread by freezing it. After baking, allow the bread to come to room temperature and then securely wrap in plastic and place inside of a zip-close freezer bag. To thaw, allow bread to come to room temperature and then reheat for 15 minutes in a 300°F oven. Thaw solidly frozen bread in a 300°F oven for 25–40 minutes, then unwrap and continue baking until heated through, 5–15 minutes more.

Focaccia

MAKES 12 SERVINGS

Focaccia is an Italian bread of great versatility and typically made with a great amount of olive oil. Our version omits the oil—yet the flavor is still delicious.

1 envelope active dry yeast
1 cup minus 1 tablespoon warm (105–115°F) water
2 cups + 2 tablespoons all-purpose flour
2 tablespoons whole-wheat flour
1 teaspoon salt

1. In a small bowl, sprinkle the yeast over the water. Let stand until foamy, about 10 minutes.

2. In a food processor, combine the all-purpose flour, whole-wheat flour, and salt. With the machine running, scrape the yeast mixture through the feed tube just until the dough forms a ball. Knead the dough by pulsing 30 times; the dough will still be sticky.

3. Spray a large bowl with nonstick cooking spray; put the dough in the bowl. Cover tightly with plastic wrap and let the dough rise in a warm, draft-free place until it doubles in size, about 1 hour.

4. Spray a baking sheet with nonstick spray. Punch down the dough. Flour your hands and form the dough into a ball. Place it on the baking sheet and press into a 10-inch circle. Cover loosely with plastic wrap and let it rise in a warm, draft-free place until it doubles in size, about 30 minutes.

5. When the dough has risen, preheat the oven to 425°F. Without piercing the dough, make dimples all over it with your fingertips. Bake on the center oven rack until browned, 15–20 minutes. Serve warm or at room temperature.

Per serving (1/12 of bread): 116 Cal, 2 g Fat, 0 g Sat Fat, 1 mg Chol, 208 mg Sod, 22 g Carb, 1 g Fib, 4 g Prot, 27 mg Calc. **POINTS: 2.**

SMART TIP

Focaccia is the perfect foil for any variety of toppings. Try herbs, such as fresh rosemary or oregano, kosher salt, chopped sun-dried tomatoes, or thinly sliced onions or olives.

Buttermilk, Fennel, and Raisin Corn Bread

MAKES 12 SERVINGS

The buttermilk in this recipe gives the corn bread a tangy flavor, while the raisins and fennel add sweetness and depth to this Southern classic. Although we baked ours in a pan, you can also use a more traditional cast-iron skillet. Spray the skillet with nonstick spray and preheat in the oven ten minutes before adding the batter. Handle the hot pan carefully!

1   cup all-purpose
     flour
¾   cup yellow
     cornmeal
1   teaspoon baking
     powder
½   teaspoon salt
¼   teaspoon baking
     soda
1   cup low-fat
     buttermilk
2   large eggs
3   tablespoons corn oil
1   cup golden raisins
1½   teaspoons fennel
     seeds

1. Preheat the oven to 425°F. Spray an 8-inch square baking dish or 10-inch cast-iron skillet with nonstick spray.

2. Combine the flour, cornmeal, baking powder, salt, and baking soda in a large bowl. Whisk together the buttermilk, eggs, and oil in medium bowl. Add the buttermilk mixture to the flour mixture; stir until blended. Stir in the raisins and fennel seeds. Using a rubber spatula, transfer the batter to the baking dish or skillet and spread evenly. Bake until golden around the edges and a toothpick inserted in the center comes out clean, 25–28 minutes.

Per serving (1⁄12 of bread): 161 Cal, 5 g Fat, 1 g Sat Fat, 37 mg Chol, 196 mg Sod, 26 g Carb, 1 g Fib, 4 g Prot, 61 mg Calc. **POINTS: 3.**

SMART TIP

This recipe easily transforms into a savory bread. Just add a pinch of cumin or chili powder, a sprinkling of chopped fresh cilantro, and/or a handful of seeded and chopped bell peppers or grilled corn kernels to the batter.

sweets & baked goods

Potato-Yogurt Bread

MAKES 16 SERVINGS

Pureed potato and yogurt keep this golden, slightly sour bread moist and dense. To get the best texture, use a baking potato (such as an Idaho or a russet), which is high in starch and low in moisture. Puree the potatoes with a food mill or ricer to get the smoothest puree—not a food processor, which will make the potato gluey in texture. Avoid using waxy potatoes with less starch and more moisture, such as red bliss or Yukon gold.

1 baking potato (about 9 ounces), peeled and quartered
1 cup plain low-fat yogurt
¼ cup warm (105–115°F) water
2¼ teaspoons honey
2 envelopes active dry yeast
2 teaspoons nonfat dry milk
4 cups + 2 tablespoons bread flour
½ cup whole-wheat flour
2 teaspoons salt

1. Place the potato and enough water to cover it in a saucepan; bring to a boil. Reduce the heat and simmer, covered, until the potato is tender, about 15 minutes. Drain and return the potato to the pan. Place over low heat and let steam-dry about 5 minutes, shaking the pan occasionally. Puree the hot potato using a ricer or food mill, and let cool to room temperature.

2. Combine the yogurt, water, honey, yeast, and dry milk in a large bowl. Stir in the potato, bread flour, whole-wheat flour, and salt until the dough starts to gather around the spoon. Turn out the dough on a work surface; knead until dough is smooth and elastic, about 5 minutes. Add more bread flour, 1 tablespoon at a time, if the dough is too wet.

3. Spray a large bowl with nonstick spray; put the dough in the bowl. Cover tightly with plastic wrap and let the dough rise in a warm, draft-free place until it doubles in size and holds an impression for a few seconds when pressed with a finger, about 1 hour.

4. Turn out the dough on a lightly floured counter. Deflate the dough by kneading it briefly. Shape the dough into a loaf, cover with plastic wrap, and let it rise 30 minutes in a warm, draft-free place.

5. Preheat the oven to 350°F. Place the loaf on a baking sheet, make a few shallow slashes across the top, and bake until the crust is golden brown and the loaf sounds hollow when tapped on the bottom, about 45 minutes. Cool completely on a rack before serving.

Per serving (¹⁄₁₆ of bread): 162 Cal, 1 g Fat, 0 g Sat Fat, 1 mg Chol, 304 mg Sod, 32 g Carb, 2 g Fib, 6 g Prot, 39 mg Calc. **POINTS: 3.**

SMART TIP
You can knead this dough by hand or in the bowl of an electric mixer fitted with a dough hook at medium speed.

Tomato-Herb Rolls

These flavorful rolls are perfect served with soup or salad. Freeze half the batch for future meals.

2 cups boiling water

12 sun-dried tomato halves (not oil-packed), cut into slivers

1 envelope active dry yeast

1¼ cups warm (105–115°F) water

3½ cups all-purpose flour

1½ teaspoons salt

2 teaspoons minced fresh rosemary, or 1 teaspoon dried

2 teaspoons minced fresh sage, or ½ teaspoon dried

½ teaspoon dried oregano

Freshly ground pepper, to taste

1 egg white, beaten with 2 teaspoons water

1. In a small bowl, pour the boiling water over the tomatoes. Let stand about 5 minutes; drain well.

2. In another small bowl, sprinkle the yeast over the warm water. Let stand until foamy, about 10 minutes.

3. In a food processor, combine the flour and salt. With the machine running, scrape the yeast mixture through the feed tube just until the dough forms a ball. Knead the dough by pulsing until it is smooth and no longer sticky, about 30 times.

4. Spray a large bowl with nonstick spray; put the dough in the bowl. Cover tightly with plastic wrap and let the dough rise in a warm, draft-free place until it doubles in size, about 1 hour.

5. Punch down the dough; lightly sprinkle a work surface with flour. Turn out the dough; knead in the tomatoes, herbs, and pepper until they are evenly distributed. Divide the dough into 12 pieces, forming each into an oval with tapered ends.

6. Spray a baking sheet with nonstick spray; place the rolls 3 inches apart on the sheet. Cover loosely with plastic wrap and let them rise in a warm, draft-free place until they double in size, about 1 hour.

7. Preheat the oven to 400°F. Bake on the center rack about 20 minutes; brush with the egg white mixture. Bake until the rolls are golden brown and sound hollow when tapped on the bottom, 3–5 minutes more. Remove from the baking sheet and cool completely on a rack.

Per serving (1 roll): 56 Cal, 0 g Fat, 0 g Sat Fat, 0 mg Chol, 342 mg Sod, 12 g Carb, 1 g Fib, 2 g Prot, 11 mg Calc. **POINTS: 1.**

SMART TIP

Rather have a loaf? After kneading in the tomatoes, herbs, and pepper in Step 5, pat the dough into a 16 x 12-inch rectangle. Fold lengthwise into thirds; pinch the seams to seal, and then form into a 16-inch loaf with tapered ends. Transfer to a baking sheet sprayed with nonstick spray and bake as directed.

Mosaic Fruit Sorbet

MAKES 8 SERVINGS

This easy dessert takes only a few minutes to assemble. But plan ahead: The sorbet needs to freeze thoroughly. To soften sorbet, place it in the refrigerator for 20–30 minutes.

1 pint mango sorbet, softened slightly

2 cups strawberries, hulled and left whole

1 ripe mango, peeled and cut into ½-inch cubes (about 1 cup)

2 kiwi fruit, peeled and cut into ½-inch cubes (about 1 cup)

2 tablespoons flaked coconut, chopped

2 tablespoons honey

1 pint raspberry sorbet, softened slightly

1. Line a 9 x 5-inch loaf pan with plastic wrap so the plastic wrap hangs over the sides of the pan (see "Smart Tip", below). Spread the softened mango sorbet into the bottom of the pan and cover with plastic wrap. Freeze until firm, 2–3 hours. 2. Cut the bottom off each strawberry so it stands upright. Arrange the strawberries on top of the mango sorbet, spacing the berries about 1½ inches apart. Combine the mango, kiwi fruit, coconut, and honey in a bowl. Spoon the fruit mixture on top of the strawberries. Spread the raspberry sorbet over the fruit, spreading the sorbet to the edges of the pan, and cover with plastic wrap. Freeze until firm, 2–3 hours or overnight. 3. To serve, uncover sorbet and invert the pan onto a serving plate. Remove the plastic wrap and cut the sorbet into slices.

Per serving (1-inch-thick slice): 178 Cal, 1 g Fat, 0 g Sat Fat, 0 mg Chol, 8 mg Sod, 44 g Carb, 3 g Fib, 1 g Prot, 14 mg Calc. **POINTS: 3.**

SMART TIP

Sprinkle the sides and bottom of a loaf pan with a few drops of water, then line it with plastic; this will make it easier to turn the sorbet onto a serving plate.

weight watchers

Frosty Green Grape Sorbet

MAKES 6 SERVINGS

As an alternative, use seedless red grapes and red grape juice, or make both kinds and serve them together. Make sure to thoroughly wash and blot grapes dry before using. Put aside a few grapes and frost them (see box "Frosty Good," below) to use as a garnish along with a few mint sprigs.

¼ cup sugar
¼ cup water
3 pounds seedless green grapes, washed and stemmed
¾ cup white grape juice
¼ cup light corn syrup
1 tablespoon grated lime rind

1. Combine the sugar and water in a saucepan and bring to a boil. Transfer the sugar syrup to a bowl and set aside.
2. Puree the grapes in a food processor. Add the grape juice, corn syrup, lime rind, and sugar syrup; pulse until combined.
3. Pour the mixture into a 9 x 13-inch metal baking pan, or a shallow plastic container and cover with plastic wrap or a lid. Freeze until the sorbet is partially frozen, about 4 hours.
4. Transfer the mixture to a food processor and pulse until almost smooth. Do not overprocess. Return the sorbet to the pan, cover, and freeze until firm, about 4 hours. Let the sorbet stand at room temperature 10 minutes to soften before serving.

Per serving (1¼ cups): 238 Cal, 1 g Fat, 0 g Sat Fat, 0 mg Chol, 21 mg Sod, 61 g Carb, 2 g Fib, 2 g Prot, 28 mg Calc. **POINTS: 4.**

SMART TIP

Freezing sorbet or granita in a shallow container allows it to freeze quickly. The deeper the container, the longer it will take to freeze. Use only metal pans or plastic containers when freezing; glass or ceramic may crack.

FROSTY GOOD

To frost grapes, rinse and blot dry. Mix equal parts egg white powder—also known as meringue powder (found in the baking section of most supermarkets)—and warm water. Lightly brush the egg white mixture onto the grapes. Sprinkle the grapes with enough sugar to lightly coat them, then let the grapes dry on wax paper until the sugar hardens into a crunchy coating, about 45–60 minutes.

Vanilla-Almond Tortoni Sorbet

This much-loved Italian frozen dessert is usually made with heavy cream or ice cream. But you can say ciao to the calories, because our version is made with fat-free vanilla frozen yogurt and part-skim ricotta cheese.

1 (8-ounce) container part-skim ricotta cheese
½ cup confectioners' sugar
1 teaspoon vanilla extract
¼ teaspoon almond extract
⅛ teaspoon ground nutmeg
2 pints fat-free vanilla frozen yogurt, softened
Nutmeg (optional)
Toasted almonds (optional)

1. Combine the ricotta, sugar, vanilla, almond extract, and the nutmeg in a food processor. Pulse until the mixture is smooth, about 5 seconds. Add the frozen yogurt and pulse to combine, about 5 seconds longer.
2. Transfer the mixture to a 9 x 13-inch metal baking pan, or a shallow plastic tub and cover with plastic wrap or a lid. Freeze until partially frozen, about 3 hours.
3. Line a 12-cup muffin tin with foil liners.
4. Transfer the mixture to a food processor and pulse until almost smooth. Do not overprocess. Spoon the mixture into the cups, cover, and freeze until firm, about 3 hours longer. Let stand at room temperature 10 minutes to soften and sprinkle with additional nutmeg and almonds (if using) before serving.

Per serving (½ cup): 100 Cal, 2 g Fat, 1 g Sat Fat, 6 mg Chol, 54 mg Sod, 18 g Carb, 0 g Fib, 4 g Prot, 352 mg Calc. **POINTS: 2.**

SMART TIP
Soften the frozen yogurt in the refrigerator 15–20 minutes.

Peachy-Rosemary Sundaes

MAKES 4 SERVINGS

Here's an elegant dessert that is reminiscent of the classic Peach Melba. Our version uses tangy nonfat yogurt cheese instead of ice cream. The addition of rosemary gives it a complex and unexpected flavor that you would expect to find in gourmet ice cream.

6   medium peaches, halved
1½ cups fresh raspberries
¼   cup orange juice
3   teaspoons sugar
2   tablespoons finely chopped fresh rosemary
1½ tablespoons orange liqueur
2   teaspoons raspberry- or rosemary-flavored vinegar
1½ cups nonfat yogurt cheese*
Fresh rosemary sprigs (optional)

1. Combine the peaches, raspberries, orange juice, 1½ teaspoons of the sugar, 1 tablespoon of the rosemary, the liqueur, and vinegar in a bowl; toss gently. Cover and set aside.

2. Combine the yogurt cheese with the remaining 1½ teaspoons sugar and the 1 tablespoon rosemary in another bowl. Divide the mixture evenly into 4 stemmed glasses or dessert cups; divide the fruit mixture evenly over the cheese. Garnish with fresh rosemary sprigs (if using). Serve chilled or at room temperature.

*To prepare yogurt cheese, spoon 3 cups plain nonfat yogurt into a coffee filter or cheesecloth-lined strainer; place over a bowl. Refrigerate, covered, at least 5 hours or overnight. Discard the liquid in the bowl. Makes 1½ cups yogurt cheese.

Per serving (1 sundae): 223 Cal, 1 g Fat, 0 g Sat Fat, 3 mg Chol, 141 mg Sod, 42 g Carb, 6 g Fib, 12 g Prot, 388 mg Calc. **POINTS: 4.**

SMART TIP

When using rosemary or any fresh herb sprig as a garnish for a dessert or drink, dip the sprig in ice water and shake off the excess. Then coat the sprig with granulated sugar, shaking off excess and placing on wax paper; freeze 30 minutes. Not only does it make an attractive garnish, it becomes a flavorful breath-freshener, or swizzle stick.

Pavlova with Fresh Berry Filling

MAKES 12 SERVINGS

This spectacular fruit-filled meringue cake is considered a national dish of Australia, though New Zealanders claim they made it first, using a different name. Created to honor the Russian ballerina Anna Pavlova, who visited both countries in 1926, the dessert has swirls of white meringue that are said to resemble her tutu. The cake is crisp on the outside and marshmallowy-soft on the inside—a perfect foil for whatever berry is in season. You can bake the Pavlova up to a day ahead; store it in an airtight container at room temperature. Fill it with the cream and berries just before serving.

1 cup sugar
6 egg whites
1½ teaspoons cornstarch
1 teaspoon distilled white vinegar
1 teaspoon vanilla extract
¼ cup boiling water
1 cup light whipped topping
½ cup nonfat sour cream
4 cups fresh berries

1. Place the oven rack in the center of the oven; preheat the oven to 350°F. Line a baking sheet with foil.

2. Whirl the sugar in a food processor or blender 2 minutes to finely grind it; set aside.

3. With an electric mixer on medium speed, beat together the egg whites, sugar, cornstarch, vinegar, and vanilla in a large bowl until combined, 1 minute. Pour in the boiling water and beat on high speed until stiff, glossy peaks form, about 5 minutes. Spread the meringue into a 10-inch circle on the baking sheet, mounding it slightly higher along the edges.

4. Place the Pavlova in the oven and immediately lower the heat to 325°F. Bake 10 minutes. Reduce the oven heat to 200°F and continue baking, 45 minutes more. Turn off the oven and let the Pavlova stand in the oven, 1 hour. Transfer to a rack and cool completely. Carefully remove the foil from the bottom of the Pavlova and transfer to a serving platter.

5. Combine the whipped topping and sour cream in a medium bowl; spread in the center of the Pavlova. Arrange the berries over the cream. To serve, use a large spoon. Each portion should include some crisp outer shell as well as the soft inner filling and berries.

Per serving (about 1 cup): 116 Cal, 1 g Fat, 1 g Sat Fat, 0 mg Chol, 43 mg Sod, 25 g Carb, 1 g Fib, 3 g Prot, 33 mg Calc. **POINTS: 2.**

SMART TIP

If your Pavlova "weeps" in the oven, you are overcooking it. The bonds between the proteins in the egg whites tighten when they are cooked too much, squeezing out water in the process. To avoid a weeping Pavlova, turn off the oven after 45 minutes, even if the dessert doesn't appear done; it will crisp as it sits in the cooling oven and even more when it cools on the rack.

Blackberry Slump

MAKES 8 SERVINGS

Slumps, and their close cousins, grunts, are descendants of steamed fruit puddings. Slumps are cooked in a covered pan with the dumplings on top.

1 cup all-purpose flour
3 tablespoons +
⅔ cup sugar
1¼ teaspoons baking powder
½ teaspoon salt
¼ teaspoon baking soda
½ teaspoon cinnamon
½ cup fat-free buttermilk
2 tablespoons unsalted butter, melted
2 pints fresh blackberries
⅓ cup water
1 tablespoon fresh lemon juice

1. Combine the flour, 3 tablespoons sugar, the baking powder, salt, baking soda, and ¼ teaspoon of the cinnamon in a medium bowl. Stir in the buttermilk and butter. Mix until a soft, sticky dough forms; set aside.

2. In a heavy 10-inch skillet (preferably cast-iron), combine the blackberries, the remaining ⅔ cup sugar, the water, lemon juice, and remaining ¼ teaspoon cinnamon; bring to a boil. Reduce the heat and simmer, uncovered, 2 minutes.

3. Spoon the dough by tablespoons onto the fruit. Cover and simmer until the dough is firm to the touch, 8–10 minutes.

Per serving (about ½ cup): 208 Cal, 4 g Fat, 2 g Sat Fat, 8 mg Chol, 255 mg Sod, 43 g Carb, 4 g Fib, 3 g Prot, 58 mg Calc. **POINTS: 4.**

SMART TIP

Although blackberries are delicious, apples, pears, or berries of any kind make a scrumptious substitution.

Fruited Rice Pudding

MAKES 8 SERVINGS

This creamy, rich home-style treat is a favorite dessert all over Latin America.

2 cups milk
1¾ cups water
½ cup uncooked white rice
½ teaspoon salt
⅓ cup sugar
1 teaspoon vanilla extract
1 large mango, peeled and chopped
1½ cups chopped pineapple

Combine 1 cup of the milk, the water, rice, and salt in a saucepan. Bring the mixture to a boil, reduce the heat, cover, and simmer 30 minutes. Stir in the remaining 1 cup of the milk, the sugar, and vanilla. Cover the saucepan and return to a simmer. Cook, stirring occasionally, until creamy, about 25 minutes. Remove from the heat, stir in the mango and pineapple, and let stand 5 minutes. Serve warm, at room temperature, or chilled.

Per serving (½ cup): 148 Cal, 2 g Fat, 1 g Sat Fat, 8 mg Chol, 176 mg Sod, 29 g Carb, 1 g Fib, 3 g Prot, 79 mg Calc. **POINTS: 3.**

SMART TIP

You can substitute papaya for the mango if it's more readily available.

Golden Delicious Phyllo Apple Tart

MAKES 10 SERVINGS

With a natural sweetness and firm but tender texture, the Golden Delicious is the perfect apple for this luscious tart.

1 lemon
5 large Golden Delicious apples, peeled, cored, and cut into 12 wedges each
½ cup granulated sugar
½ cup packed dark brown sugar
1 teaspoon cinnamon
½ teaspoon freshly grated nutmeg
¼ cup hazelnuts, toasted, skins removed, and chopped
1 tablespoon apple brandy or Grand Marnier
3 tablespoons unsalted butter
4 tablespoons apple jelly
1 tablespoon water
9 (12 x 17-inch) sheets phyllo dough, thawed according to package directions

1. Adjust the rack to divide the oven in half; preheat the oven to 350°F. Grate the rind from the lemon; set aside. Cut lemon in half and squeeze enough juice to measure 2 tablespoons.
2. Combine the lemon juice, apples, granulated sugar, brown sugar, cinnamon, and nutmeg in a large nonstick skillet over medium heat. Simmer, stirring to dissolve the sugar, until the apples are golden brown, about 10 minutes. With a slotted spoon, transfer the apples to a bowl. Pour the syrup into a small bowl, cover, and refrigerate. Add the hazelnuts, lemon rind, and brandy to the apples. Stir to combine, then cool.
3. Combine the butter, 3 tablespoons of the apple jelly, and the water in a microwavable bowl. Microwave on High until melted, about 30 seconds; stir to blend. Carefully remove the phyllo sheets from the package, arrange in a flat stack, and cover with plastic wrap to retain moisture. With a pastry brush, lightly coat one sheet with the butter-jelly mixture, and then fold it into thirds lengthwise, lightly coating each new surface as you fold it. Lay the strip in a 9-inch square pie pan, with one end of the strip at the base of the side of the pan and the other end hanging over the opposite edge. Repeat with the remaining butter-jelly mixture and phyllo sheets, overlapping the strips in the pan in spoke-wheel fashion so that the entire inside surface of the pan is covered.
4. Spread the remaining 1 tablespoon of jelly over the phyllo in the pan. Spoon the apples evenly over the jelly, then fold the overhanging portion of each strip of phyllo toward the center of the pan and twist to form a rosette. The phyllo will not cover the center of the tart and most of the filling will show.
5. Place the tart on a baking sheet and bake in the center of the oven until nicely browned, about 45 minutes. Serve warm or at room temperature with the reserved syrup drizzled over the top.

Per serving (¹⁄₁₀ of tart): 257 Cal, 7 g Fat, 3 g Sat Fat, 10 mg Chol, 90 mg Sod, 48 g Carb, 2 g Fib, 2 g Prot, 26 mg Calc. **POINTS: 5.**

SMART TIP

For easy clean up, line the baking sheet with parchment or foil.

Pumpkin Custard with Caramelized Pecans

MAKES 8 SERVINGS

Although pumpkins are available fresh from early fall through late winter, most cooks prefer the convenience of canned pumpkin, reserving the fresh variety mostly for carving Halloween jack-o'-lanterns and toasting their seeds.

⅓ cup sugar

2 tablespoons water

1 cup pecan halves

2 cups low-fat (1%) milk

½ teaspoon cinnamon

¼ teaspoon ground cardamom

¼ teaspoon ground cloves

½ cup packed light brown sugar

4 large eggs

2 egg whites

⅔ cup canned pumpkin puree

1 teaspoon vanilla extract

1. Preheat the oven to 350°F. Arrange eight 6-ounce custard cups in a large roasting pan.

2. Combine the sugar and water in a saucepan; bring to a boil. Cook, without stirring, until the sugar turns a light caramel color, about 5 minutes. Stir in the pecans and toss to coat. Cook until the mixture is a dark caramel color, about 3 minutes more. Quickly pour the pecan mixture onto a large nonstick baking sheet and cool completely on a rack. Break the nut mixture into small pieces and sprinkle into the custard cups. Set aside.

3. Combine the milk, cinnamon, cardamom, and cloves in a saucepan and bring to a boil. Cook, stirring occasionally, 2 minutes. Whisk the brown sugar, eggs, and egg whites in a large bowl. Whisk the hot milk mixture into the egg mixture. Stir in the pumpkin and vanilla. Ladle the mixture into the custard cups.

4. Place the roasting pan in the oven, then pour enough hot water into the pan to come halfway up the sides of the custard cups. Bake until a knife inserted in the center of the custards comes out clean, about 30 minutes. Remove the cups from the roasting pan and cool on a rack. Cover and refrigerate at least 4 hours before serving.

Per serving (1 custard): 249 Cal, 12 g Fat, 2 g Sat Fat, 109 mg Chol, 83 mg Sod, 29 g Carb, 2 g Fib, 7 g Prot, 112 mg Calc. **POINTS: 6.**

SMART TIP

For ease, use a tea kettle in Step 4 to pour the hot water into the roasting pan.

Rosy Pear Upside-Down Cake

MAKES 8 SERVINGS

This wonderfully moist cake should always be served warm, if you are to best appreciate its sticky-sweet topping. Select ripe but firm pears; they'll hold their shape well in cooking.

TOPPING

- 1 tablespoon unsalted butter
- ¼ cup seedless raspberry or strawberry jam
- 2 drops red food coloring (optional)
- 2 ripe, firm pears (14 ounces), peeled, halved, and cored

CAKE

- 1½ cups all-purpose flour
- 1 teaspoon baking powder
- ½ teaspoon baking soda
- 1 teaspoon ground cardamom
- ½ teaspoon ground ginger
- ¼ teaspoon salt
- ⅔ cup sugar
- 3 tablespoons unsalted butter, melted and cooled
- 1 large egg
- 2 teaspoons vanilla extract
- ⅔ cup plain nonfat yogurt

1. Place the oven rack in the lower third of the oven; preheat to 375°F. Spray a 9-inch round cake pan with nonstick spray.
2. Place the butter in a microwavable cup measure; cover with plastic wrap. Microwave on High until melted, 20–30 seconds. Stir in the jam and food coloring (if using) until blended. Spoon in the center of the prepared pan, spreading evenly (it's not necessary to spread all the way to the edge of the pan).
3. Place a pear half cut-side down onto a work surface, and cut lengthwise into ⅛-inch slices. Invert, cut-side up, onto your palm or a spatula. Press down lightly to fan out the slices, and place in the prepared pan with the stem towards the center. Repeat with the remaining pear halves, arranging the slices to overlap slightly. Arrange any smaller pieces in the center. Bake until the pears are almost tender, 15–20 minutes.
4. Meanwhile, whisk the flour, baking powder, baking soda, cardamom, ginger, and salt in a medium bowl and set aside.
5. Whisk together the sugar, butter, egg, and vanilla in a medium bowl until smooth; whisk in the yogurt. Add the flour mixture and stir just until combined; do not overmix.
6. Drop the batter by spoonfuls over the hot topping. (Don't worry about covering the topping; the batter will spread as it bakes.) Bake until the top of the cake springs back when lightly pressed and a toothpick inserted in the center comes out clean, 25–30 minutes. Let stand 3 minutes; run a knife around the edge. Invert onto a serving platter, using potholders, and gently shake the pan to loosen. Remove the pan; let cool 15 minutes and serve warm.

Per serving (⅛ of cake): 278 Cal, 7 g Fat, 4 g Sat Fat, 43 mg Chol, 229 mg Sod, 49 g Carb, 2 g Fib, 5 g Prot, 65 mg Calc. **POINTS: 6.**

SMART TIP

You can make this cake up to two days ahead; refrigerate, wrapped well in plastic. Before serving, cover with foil and reheat at 325°F, for 15–20 minutes, or until warmed through.

Lemony Pizzelle

MAKES 20 SERVINGS

Pizzelle, Italian for "little pizzas," are crispy, wafflelike cookies made on a specially designed iron (see box, "Kitchen Aides," below). Beautiful to look at, they provide plenty of satisfying crunch—with only a little fat.

- 4 egg whites
- 2 large eggs
- 1½ cups sugar
- 2 tablespoons grated lemon rind (from 2 lemons)
- ¼ cup fresh lemon juice
- 3 tablespoons canola or light olive oil
- 2 tablespoons unsalted butter, melted
- ¼ teaspoon salt
- 3 cups all-purpose flour

1. With an electric mixer on medium speed, beat the egg whites, eggs, sugar, and lemon rind in a large bowl until pale yellow and thickened, about 5 minutes. Add the lemon juice, oil, butter, and salt; reduce the speed to low and beat just until combined. Add the flour and beat just until combined; do not overbeat. (The mixture should be the consistency of cake batter.)

2. Preheat the pizzelle iron according to manufacturer's instructions. Spray lightly with nonstick spray. Drop the batter by slightly rounded tablespoonfuls into the center of each pattern and spread evenly with the back of a spoon. Close the iron, pressing down to evenly distribute the batter. Bake until golden, 40–70 seconds.

3. Remove with a heatproof spatula and cool on a rack. Repeat with the remaining batter, lightly spraying with nonstick spray between batches.

Per serving (2 pizzelles): 166 Cal, 4 g Fat, 1 g Sat Fat, 25 mg Chol, 47 mg Sod, 29 g Carb, 1 g Fib, 3 g Prot, 7 mg Calc. **POINTS: 3.**

SMART TIP

Store the pizzelles in an airtight container for two weeks, or freeze for up to two months.

KITCHEN AIDES

You may not need another kitchen gadget, but once you savor the beautiful, lacy goodness of a homemade pizzelle, you'll be convinced you need a pizzelle iron. They're available in larger kitchenware stores, especially during the holiday season.

Mocha Angel Food Cake

MAKES 12 SERVINGS

Serve this mile-high cake with fresh berries or sprigs of fresh mint. Because angel food cake relies solely on beaten egg whites to give it height, don't overmix the batter. Be sure to pop it in the oven as soon as you've prepared the batter.

- 2 ounces bittersweet or semisweet chocolate
- 1 cup granulated sugar
- ½ cup packed light brown sugar
- 1 cup sifted cake flour
- 2 tablespoons unsweetened cocoa powder, sifted
- 1½ tablespoons fine instant coffee granules
- ½ teaspoon salt
- 12 egg whites, room temperature
- 1 teaspoon cream of tartar, or 2 teaspoons lemon juice
- 1½ teaspoons vanilla extract

1. Place the oven rack in the lower third of the oven; preheat to 325°F. Set a 10 x 4-inch straight-sided tube pan nearby.

2. Chop the chocolate into small pieces with a sharp heavy knife, none larger than ¼ inch. (There will be smaller chips and crumbs; this is fine.) Set aside. In a food processor or blender, process the granulated sugar and brown sugar until finely ground, about 2 minutes, working in 2 batches, if necessary.

3. Sift the flour, cocoa, instant coffee, salt, and ¾ cup of the sugar mixture in a medium bowl.

4. With an electric mixer on low speed, beat the egg whites in a large bowl until frothy, about 2 minutes. Add the cream of tartar and beat until soft and fluffy, about 2 minutes. Increase the speed to medium and beat in the remaining sugar mixture, 1 tablespoon at a time, until shiny, soft peaks form; do not overbeat. Beat in the vanilla.

5. Sprinkle 4 rounded tablespoons of the flour mixture over the batter. Using a large rubber spatula, gently fold in the flour mixture, until almost combined. Repeat, adding the chopped chocolate with the last addition of flour. Spoon into the pan and spread evenly.

6. Bake immediately, until the top springs back when firmly pressed, 55–65 minutes. Invert onto a bottleneck or inverted metal funnel and cool completely, 2–3 hours. To loosen the cake, run a thin-bladed knife around the edges of the pan and center tube. Invert onto a plate or cake rack, then reinvert, right-side up.

Per serving (¹⁄₁₂ of cake): 175 Cal, 2 g Fat, 1 g Sat Fat, 0 mg Chol, 157 mg Sod, 36 g Carb, 1 g Fib, 5 g Prot, 15 mg Calc. **POINTS: 3.**

SMART TIP

The instant coffee should be finely granulated; if you have instant coffee crystals, crush them between sheets of wax paper, using the bottom of a small heavy skillet. The cake can be made ahead: Wrap well in plastic wrap and store at room temperature up to four days, or freeze for up to two weeks.

THE YEAR IN CHOCOLATE

**If you thought chocolate for dessert was
on the list of diet no-nos, give our
sinfully delicious chocolate treats a taste.**

Chocolate Crispy Bars

MAKES 24 SERVINGS

Admit it. You love those chewy, marshmallowy bars made with crisped rice, though they do seem overly sweet now that you're out of grade school. This grown-up version of the classic treat tempers its sweetness with real chocolate flavor. Although the squares are best served the day they are made, they'll keep in an airtight container for up to three days.

2 tablespoons unsalted butter

1 ounce unsweetened chocolate, finely chopped

1 (7-ounce) jar marshmallow cream

2 tablespoons unsweetened Dutch-process cocoa powder

1 teaspoon vanilla extract

6 cups crisped rice cereal

1. Spray a 9 x 13-inch baking pan with nonstick spray.

2. Melt the butter and chocolate in a large saucepan over low heat. Add the marshmallow cream, cocoa, and vanilla; stir until smooth. Remove from heat and add the cereal, stirring until well coated.

3. Spread the mixture into the prepared pan. Spray your hands with nonstick spray and press the batter down evenly. Let cool 10 minutes, then cut into 24 squares.

Per serving (1 square): 69 Cal, 2 g Fat, 1 g Sat Fat, 3 mg Chol, 77 mg Sod, 13 g Carb, 1 g Fib, 1 g Prot, 3 mg Calc. **POINTS: 1.**

SMART TIP

Chocolate can crumble excessively when it is chopped. To keep track of the crumbs, use a good-size cutting board and a large, sharp knife. You can also grate chocolate with a cheese grater; catch the gratings in a bowl.

HOT CHOCOLATE!

There are plenty of reasons why chocolate could make your heart happily flutter: A recent study at the University of Scranton, in Pennsylvania, found that chocolate is rich in polyphenols, the plant antioxidants that may play a role in preventing heart disease and some cancers. The darker the chocolate, the better: The amount of polyphenols in a typical 1.4-ounce serving of dark chocolate is equivalent to that in a cup of black tea and higher than that in a glass of red wine. And though the fat in cocoa butter is highly saturated, it's mainly comprised of stearic acid, a fat that doesn't seem to affect blood cholesterol either way.

Of course, all these benefits must be balanced with chocolate's role as a source of calories: 1 ounce of bittersweet still adds up to about 155 calories (or 4 **POINTS**). But it does show that indulging in a little chocolate is indeed treating yourself with love.

Rum Truffles

MAKES 24 SERVINGS

These intensely flavored confections make the perfect Valentine's Day gift—but be sure to save some for yourself! They'll keep for up to a week in an airtight container, or up to a month in the freezer.

¼ cup semisweet chocolate chips
2 ounces Neufchâtel cheese
¼ teaspoon imitation rum extract
2 cups confectioners' sugar, sifted
2 tablespoons unsweetened Dutch-process cocoa powder

1. Microwave the chocolate chips in a medium microwavable bowl on High until nearly melted, 30–45 seconds; stir until smooth. Let cool.

2. Add the cheese and rum extract; with an electric mixer on medium speed, beat until smooth, 1 minute. Add the sugar, and continue beating until smooth and thick. Shape the mixture into a thin, 12-inch log. Wrap well in plastic, and refrigerate until chilled through, at least 30 minutes.

3. Spread the cocoa onto a sheet of wax paper. Slice the log into 24 pieces and roll each into a ¾-inch ball. Roll the balls in the cocoa to evenly coat.

Per serving (1 truffle): 55 Cal, 1 g Fat, 1 g Sat Fat, 2 mg Chol, 10 mg Sod, 11 g Carb, 0 g Fib, 0 g Prot, 3 mg Calc. **POINTS: 1.**

SMART TIP

For a yummy variation, substitute ¼ teaspoon peppermint extract or ⅛ teaspoon coconut extract for the rum extract.

Cocoa Roll with Creamy Mint Filling

MAKES 12 SERVINGS

If you've never made a jelly-roll style cake before, this recipe is a great one to try.

COCOA ROLL

⅓ cup all-purpose flour

¼ cup + 2 teaspoons unsweetened cocoa powder

¼ teaspoon baking soda

¼ teaspoon salt

4 large eggs (room temperature), separated

1 teaspoon vanilla extract

¾ cup sugar

CREAMY MINT FILLING

1 envelope (½ package) whipped topping mix

½ cup low-fat (1%) milk

¾ cup marshmallow cream

⅛ to ¼ teaspoon peppermint extract

4 drops green food coloring

Mint sprigs (optional)

1. To prepare the cocoa roll, preheat the oven to 375°F. Line the bottom of a jelly-roll pan with wax paper and spray with nonstick spray. Sift the flour, the ¼ cup cocoa, the baking soda, and salt over another sheet of wax paper to combine.

2. With an electric mixer on high speed, beat the egg yolks and vanilla in a medium bowl until lemon colored and thickened, about 5 minutes. Add ¼ cup of the sugar, and beat until pale and thickened, 2 minutes more. Set aside.

3. With clean beaters, in another bowl, beat the egg whites at medium speed until very soft peaks form, 1–2 minutes. Gradually beat in the remaining ½ cup sugar until stiff peaks form.

4. Fold the yolk mixture and ⅓ of the cocoa mixture into the egg whites, just until combined. Fold in the remaining cocoa mixture in 2 additions, just until combined; do not overmix. Evenly spread the batter into the prepared pan. Bake until the top springs back when lightly touched, 12–14 minutes; do not overbake, or the cake will crack when rolled.

5. Meanwhile, cut a sheet of paper towel covering the length of the jelly-roll pan, and lay it on a flat surface. Lightly sift the remaining 2 teaspoons cocoa powder evenly on top. Carefully invert the hot cake onto the paper towel, and remove the wax paper. Starting with the short side, roll up the cake and set seam-side down on a rack to cool completely.

6. To prepare the filling, with mixer on medium speed, beat together the topping mix and milk in a bowl, according to package directions. Add the marshmallow cream, peppermint extract, and food coloring; beat just until combined.

7. Spread the filling over the unrolled cake to within 1 inch of the edges. Roll up the cake, place it seam-side down on a serving plate, and chill 1 hour. Using a serrated knife, slice into 12 pieces, and garnish with the mint sprigs (if using).

Per serving (⅞-inch-thick slice): 129 Cal, 2 g Fat, 1 g Sat Fat, 71 mg Chol, 105 mg Sod, 25 g Carb, 1 g Fib, 3 g Prot, 19 mg Calc. **POINTS: 3.**

SMART TIP

The cake can keep for up to three weeks; wrap in plastic wrap, place in a freezer bag, and freeze. To thaw, refrigerate wrapped cake overnight, or at room temperature for three hours.

Iced Cappuccino Smoothie

Craving something cool, creamy, and bursting with chocolate flavor? Try this rich, mocha shake, adapted from the book *Forbidden Foods Diabetic Cooking* (American Diabetes Association, 2000). You can prepare the mix in minutes—the recipe easily doubles—and store it in an airtight container in the pantry for up to three months. Just whirl a little mix with ice and milk in the blender when the smoothie mood strikes.

SMOOTHIE MIX
- ½ cup fat-free vanilla-flavored powdered coffee creamer
- ⅓ cup instant regular or decaffeinated coffee granules
- ⅓ cup instant fat-free milk powder
- ¼ cup sugar
- 2 tablespoons unsweetened Dutch-process cocoa powder

SINGLE SMOOTHIE
- ½ cup fat-free milk
- 2 tablespoons smoothie mix
- 6–8 ice cubes

1. To prepare the smoothie mix, combine the coffee creamer, coffee granules, milk powder, sugar, and cocoa in a blender, and pulse several times until finely powdered and well blended.
2. To prepare a smoothie, combine the milk and smoothie mix in blender; whirl until smooth. Add the ice cubes and pulse until thick and creamy.

Per serving (1½ cups): 114 Cal, 0 g Fat, 0 g Sat Fat, 4 mg Chol, 127 mg Sod, 20 g Carb, 1 g Fib, 9 g Prot, 297 mg Calc. **POINTS: 2.**

CHOCOLATE 101
Bewildered by all the chocolate choices these days? Here, a guide to your favorite goody.

Chocolate Liquor: A thick paste made from roasted shelled cocoa beans. The richest, most intense chocolates contain high amounts of it. Chocolate makers conch, or blend and knead, the chocolate liquor, adding other ingredients such as cocoa butter, cream, milk powder, and/or flavorings. The end result is what we call chocolate.

Cocoa Powder: The dry solids that remain when fatty cocoa butter is extracted from chocolate liquor—it has the full chocolate flavor with only a fraction of the fat. In baking, Dutch-process cocoas (also called alkalized) perform differently than nonalkalized cocoas; don't substitute them in baking unless the recipe specifically says to do so.

Unsweetened/Baking Chocolate: Pure, hardened, chocolate liquor—not meant for eating plain, but perfect for cooking and baking.

Bittersweet/Semisweet Chocolate: These terms are basically interchangeable—both refer to chocolate that is at least 35 percent chocolate liquor, with cocoa butter, sugar, emulsifiers, and other flavorings making up the rest of the ingredients.

Milk Chocolate: A mixture of at least 10 percent chocolate liquor plus milk solids, sugar, and cocoa butter.

Fudgy-Frosted Brownies

MAKES 12 SERVINGS

These chewy brownies are a chocolate lover's delight, thanks to a combination of cocoa and coffee in the batter, and an intense, fudge-like frosting. Store them in the refrigerator in an airtight container; they'll last about one week. Return them to room temperature before serving.

BROWNIES

- ¼ cup (½ stick) unsalted butter, melted and cooled
- ¾ cup packed light brown sugar
- ¾ cup granulated sugar
- ⅔ cup unsweetened applesauce
- 1 large egg
- 1 teaspoon vanilla extract
- ½ teaspoon instant coffee granules, dissolved in 1 teaspoon hot water
- ½ cup unsweetened cocoa powder
- 1 cup all-purpose flour
- ¼ teaspoon baking powder
- ½ teaspoon salt

FROSTING

- 1 teaspoon hot water
- ¼ teaspoon instant coffee granules
- 2 tablespoons corn syrup
- 2 tablespoons unsweetened cocoa powder
- ½ cup confectioners' sugar
- ½ teaspoon vanilla extract

1. To prepare the brownies, preheat the oven to 350°F. Line an 8-inch square baking pan with foil, leaving enough overhang to make two handles (see Smart Tip, below), and lightly spray with nonstick spray.

2. Whisk together the butter, brown sugar, granulated sugar, applesauce, egg, vanilla, and the dissolved coffee granules in a medium bowl until blended. Whisk in the cocoa. Add the flour, baking powder, and salt; stir with a wooden spoon just until combined. Pour into the prepared pan.

3. Bake until a pick inserted in the center comes out with a few fudgy (not raw) crumbs clinging to it, 18–22 minutes; do not overbake. Cool in the pan on a rack, 10 minutes.

4. To prepare the frosting, combine the water and instant coffee in a small saucepan until dissolved. Add the corn syrup and cook over low heat until hot but not boiling. Add the cocoa and stir until smooth. Remove from the heat and stir in the confectioners' sugar and vanilla until smooth.

5. Lift the brownies out of the pan and set on the rack. Spoon the frosting mixture over the warm brownies and spread level; cool completely. To serve, dip a serrated knife in hot water and cut into 12 pieces.

Per serving (1 brownie): 225 Cal, 5 g Fat, 3 g Sat Fat, 28 mg Chol, 124 mg Sod, 46 g Carb, 2 g Fib, 3 g Prot, 29 mg Calc. **POINTS: 5.**

SMART TIP

To make sure your brownies (or bar cookies) are easy to remove and cleanly cut, line the pan with enough foil to form handles—so you can just lift them out. (Did we mention no cleanup, either?) To line the pan, cut a piece of foil about 8 inches longer than the pan. Place the pan upside down on the foil, flip the pan over, then press the foil inside, leaving an overhang on two opposite sides.

Chocolate Wafers

These crisp-edged wafers get their deep chocolate flavor from a combination of high-quality cocoa and finely ground coffee. (Use decaf beans, if you like, but make sure to use the finest grind possible.) We like them best plain for an intense chocolate hit, but they can also turn low-fat frozen yogurt or raspberry sorbet into an elegant dessert. Another idea: Use these wafers to make bite-size low-fat ice cream sandwiches.

½ cup all-purpose flour

½ cup unsweetened Dutch-process cocoa powder

1 teaspoon finely ground regular or decaffeinated coffee

Pinch salt

2 tablespoons unsalted butter, softened

⅓ cup granulated sugar

¼ cup packed dark brown sugar

1 teaspoon vanilla extract

1 egg white

1. Whisk together the flour, cocoa, coffee, and salt in a medium bowl.

2. With an electric mixer on medium speed, beat the butter, granulated sugar, brown sugar, and vanilla in a medium bowl until fluffy, about 2 minutes. Add the egg white and beat until smooth, 1 minute more. Beat in the flour mixture until evenly blended. Shape the dough into an 8-inch log, and wrap well in plastic. Refrigerate until chilled through, at least 1 hour.

3. Preheat the oven to 350°F. Line two baking sheets with parchment or wax paper.

4. With a serrated knife, slice the log into twenty four ¼-inch-thick rounds. Arrange on the prepared baking sheets 2 inches apart and bake until firm, 8 minutes (do not over-bake; the cookies will crisp as they cool). Cool completely on a rack. Store in an airtight container for up to 1 week, or freeze up to 2 months.

Per serving (2 wafers): 85 Cal, 2 g Fat, 1 g Sat Fat, 5 mg Chol, 31 mg Sod, 16 g Carb, 1 g Fib, 2 g Prot, 10 mg Calc. **POINTS: 2.**

SMART TIP

Want to add a romantic touch for Valentine's Day? Shape the dough in Step 2 into a heart-shaped log.

S'mores

MAKES 4 SERVINGS

This campfire comfort food needn't be a calorie-fest. Our version substitutes lower-fat chips for the usual fattening chocolate bar. They're simple to use and just as ooey-gooey delicious. You can even make the S'mores in the oven; no need to wait for a camping trip. Just place the wrapped S'mores in a preheated 350°F oven on a baking sheet. They'll be ready in 7 to 8 minutes.

8 (2½-inch square) honey graham crackers

¼ cup semisweet chocolate chips

8 marshmallows (regular, not mini, size)

1. Preheat the grill for indirect heating.

2. Cut four 6-inch square pieces of aluminum foil; spray with nonstick spray. Top each piece of foil with a whole graham cracker. Top each graham cracker with 1 tablespoon of the chocolate chips, then 2 marshmallows. Place another graham cracker on top, and fold the foil tightly around each "sandwich" to seal.

3. Grill just long enough to melt the marshmallows and chocolate, 7–8 minutes.

Per serving (1 S'more): 151 Cal, 4 g Fat, 2 g Sat Fat, 0 mg Chol, 86 mg Sod, 29 g Carb, 1 g Fib, 1 g Prot, 7 mg Calc. **POINTS: 3.**

SMART TIP

For a decadent variation, make these S'mores with half peanut butter chips and half chocolate chips (you'll need 2 tablespoons of each).

A SWEET STRATEGY

There is no compromising when it comes to chocolate—even if it means limiting sugar and fat. Consider these strategies for getting the most flavor out of just a little chocolate.

■ Layer the chocolate flavor in a recipe, using a combination of different types in small amounts. Try using baking chocolate, chocolate chips, cocoa, or a chocolate frosting or glaze to build a rich chocolate taste without adding a lot of calories and fat. Coffee and cinnamon also boosts chocolate's intensity.

■ Use dark, bittersweet chocolate with a high level of cocoa solids. Anything above 50 percent (percentages are on the label) is high, which is good. The darker the chocolate, the more intense the flavor—and the less you'll need to use. Even milk chocolate fans will swoon.

■ Substitute Dutch-process (alkalized) cocoa whenever a recipe specifies to do so. With its more mellow flavor and darker color, it creates a richer, more chocolaty sensation than its American cousin. However, in baking, it will perform slightly differently.

■ Try sprinkling some chocolate chips on top of baked goods (in a recipe that calls for chips) just before you remove them from the oven. Since they're the first thing you'll taste when you take a bite, you can use less chips overall and still get a chocolate wallop in every mouthful.

INDEX

DRY AND LIQUID MEASUREMENT EQUIVALENTS

If you are converting the recipes in this magazine to metric measurements, use the following chart as a guide.

TEASPOONS	TABLESPOONS	CUPS	FLUID OUNCES
3 teaspoons	1 tablespoon		½ fluid ounce
6 teaspoons	2 tablespoons	⅛ cup	1 fluid ounce
8 teaspoons	2 tablespoons plus 2 teaspoons	⅙ cup	
12 teaspoons	4 tablespoons	¼ cup	2 fluid ounces
15 teaspoons	5 tablespoons	⅓ cup minus 1 teaspoon	2 fluid ounces
16 teaspoons	5 tablespoons plus 1 teaspoon	⅓ cup	
18 teaspoons	6 tablespoons	¼ cup plus 2 tablespoons	3 fluid ounces
24 teaspoons	8 tablespoons	½ cup	4 fluid ounces
30 teaspoons	10 tablespoons	½ cup plus 2 tablespoons	5 fluid ounces
32 teaspoons	10 tablespoons plus 2 teaspoons	⅔ cup	
36 teaspoons	12 tablespoons	¾ cup	6 fluid ounces
42 teaspoons	14 tablespoons	1 cup minus 1 tablespoon	7 fluid ounces
45 teaspoons	15 tablespoons	1 cup minus 1 tablespoon	
48 teaspoons	16 tablespoons	1 cup	8 fluid ounces

Note: Measurement of less than ⅛ teaspoon is considered a dash or a pinch.

VOLUME	
¼ teaspoon	1 milliliter
½ teaspoon	2 milliliters
1 teaspoon	5 milliliters
1 tablespoon	15 milliliters
2 tablespoons	20 milliliters
3 tablespoons	45 milliliters
¼ cup	60 milliliters
⅓ cup	75 milliliters
½ cup	125 milliliters
⅔ cup	150 milliliters
¾ cup	175 milliliters
⅔ cup	150 milliliters
1 cup	225 milliliters
1 quart	150 liters

OVEN TEMPERATURE	
250°F	120°C
275°F	140°C
300°F	150°C
325°F	160°C
350°F	180°C
375°F	190°C
400°F	200°C
425°F	220°C
450°F	230°C
475°F	250°C
500°F	260°C
525°F	270°C

WEIGHT	
1 ounce	30 grams
¼ pound	120 grams
½ pound	240 grams
¾ pound	360 grams

LENGTH	
1 inch	25 millimeters
1 inch	2.5 centimeters